MASTERING
OUTREACH &
EVANGELISM

MASTERING
OUTREACH &
EVANGELISM

Calvin Ratz
Frank Tillapaugh
Myron Augsburger

MULTNOMAH
Portland, Oregon 97266

Christianity Today, Inc.

MASTERING OUTREACH AND EVANGELISM
© 1990 by Christianity Today, Inc.
Published by Multnomah Press
Portland, Oregon 97266

Multnomah Press is a ministry of Multnomah School of the Bible, 8435 N.E. Glisan Street, Portland, Oregon 97220.

Printed in the United States of America.

Library of Congress Cataloging-in-Publication Data

Augsburger, Myron S.
  Mastering outreach and evangelism / Myron Augsburger, Calvin Ratz, Frank Tillapaugh.
      p.   cm.
  ISBN 0-88070-363-6
  1. Evangelistic work. 2. Evangelistic work—United States. I. Ratz, Calvin C. II. Tillapaugh, Frank R. III. Title.
BV3790.A79 1990
269'.2—dc20   90-35601
                                                                   CIP

94 95 96 97 98 99 - 10 9 8 7 6 5 4 3

CONTENTS

Introduction

One theologian has said that "the church exists for mission as fire exists for burning." Well, yes and no.

To be sure, the church *ought* to exist for mission. "Nowhere in the Bible is the world exhorted to 'come to church,' " says Richard Halverson. "But the church's mandate is clear. She must go to the world."

Yet statistics indicate we don't. Church sociologist Win Arn says that at least 75 percent of the congregations in America are plateaued or experiencing a decline in membership. And experience in most churches confirms the numbers. Few budgets can get passed without some group clamoring for more benevolence giving, and few in-house programs will be supported without somebody complaining about how little the church does outside its walls. Ergo, many members feel the church could or should be doing more to reach out.

And there's no use pinning the blame on reluctant lay people or lazy pastors. As these experiences show, the church is full of people who would like nothing better than to reach out to their communities and bring the Good News to the needy.

So why aren't we doing it better? Because the task is more complicated than writing systematic theology, as Emil Brunner, the theologian quoted at the beginning, would have been the first to admit. Of course, it's not so difficult that a local church can't do it. In fact, thousands are reaching out energetically and effectively. But the challenges remain.

For example, the church faces not just the obstacles society puts in our way, but some we inadvertently create, like using the same old methods in a changing environment. How do we recognize such obstacles so we don't keep playing bumper-car evangelism with them, never quite getting out to the community with our message?

Furthermore, if our people want to reach out but don't know how, in what ways should we prepare, equip, and sustain them in outreach? What is the pastor's role in making evangelism a reality? What administrative structures will encourage these vital tasks for years to come?

Further still, how can we keep these structures from becoming hollow? Exactly how does a church find its niche of service in the community? How do we integrate new people into the life of the church? What are the most effective strategies for outreach and evangelism in the 1990s?

Such are the concerns of this third volume of the *Mastering Ministry* series, and, not surprisingly, the three previous paragraphs correspond to the content of the three sections of the book: "Preparing the Way," "Structures," and "Strategies."

The title of this volume uses two words: *outreach* and *evangel-*

ism. Although the church's missionary task is one, most pastors recognize it has two interrelated components: to reach out with compassion to the needy and to proclaim the Good News of Jesus Christ to the lost. This book, then, talks about the practical aspects of sharing the love of Christ in both deed and word.

To that end, LEADERSHIP has brought together three pastors who lead churches that reach out to and evangelize their communities with love, word, and imagination.

Myron Augsburger

Myron Augsburger is a man not satisfied to serve Christ in one capacity. He's had a variety of ministry experiences and earned his share of academic degrees, including a Th.D. from Union Theological Seminary in Virginia. Presently, he pastors Washington Community Fellowship, a Mennonite congregation in inner-city Washington, D.C., and is president of the Christian College Coalition. He also writes books (such as *Evangelism as Discipling* and *I'll See You Again*) and teaches seminary courses and does itinerant evangelism when invited. Among other things.

His broad experience is matched by his calm yet bold personality. In our conversations, he spoke in a measured voice, but his fervent commitment to spreading the gospel reverberated in every word.

For example, once when he was in Canton, Ohio, for a city-wide crusade, a group of city leaders invited him to lunch. In the course of the meal, an attorney who sat across from Myron asked him bluntly, "What does a Mennonite evangelist have to offer to Canton, Ohio?"

"Come and see," Myron responded.

The lawyer, however, wasn't through. "Tell me, what do you think about sex?"

"I'm for it," Myron said.

The man then jumped up and reached his hand across the table and grabbed Myron's saying, "You're my kind of preacher."

But Myron held on to his hand and said, "But listen to me a

moment. I think too highly of sex to have it cheapened."

The table became silent. One of the attorney's colleagues turned to the sheepish lawyer and asked, "How do you answer that?"

Myron brings such courage and quiet energy to this book, and his chapters reflect his experiences in both itinerant ministry and the inner-city pastorate.

Calvin Ratz

As you stand amid the construction debris at Abbotsford Pentecostal Assembly, about an hour east of Vancouver, British Columbia, you see two things: First, nearby, rises a magnificent, state-of-the-art auditorium that will seat hundreds — people won to faith and attracted to church participation by a pastor and congregation concerned about what the Bible calls "lost sheep." Second, if you lift your eyes toward the horizon, a nearly 360-degree sweep of majestic mountain peaks in the Cascades, Olympics, and Canadian Rockies greets you. It helps you understand something of the lofty vision of Pastor Calvin Ratz.

Calvin, however, is also a down-to-earth pastor. Although his church is large and growing, although he speaks regularly at such gatherings as the Billy Graham School of Evangelism, he doesn't claim any special dispensation when it comes to evangelism.

"I have a close friend and ministerial associate," Calvin says, "who, without fail, can go to a restaurant and build a warm relationship with the waitress before she's even taken the order. And before lunch is over, he's done something to share his faith with her. I've eaten with him dozens of times and I've never seen him go into a restaurant and not do it.

"I marvel at that and wonder, *Why can't I do that?* Sharing my faith is usually a struggle for me. The other day I was in a hotel, and the maid noticed my Bible in the room. As I walked by her in the hall, she said, 'Hey, I want to talk to you. You've got a Bible.'

"Ten years ago I probably would have said, 'I'll talk to you later. I'm on my way to a meeting,' even though she was handing me the opportunity to share my faith. But this time I talked with her, though I didn't lead her to the Lord. So I'm working on my witness, but it's not happening to the extent it should."

Perhaps he's being modest. Yet, the evidence of his effectiveness has followed him for some time. Calvin has degrees from Syracuse University (M.A., Journalism), Carlton University in Ottawa (Bachelor of Commerce), and Eastern Pentecostal Bible College in Peterborough, Ontario. His ministry experience included five years in Hong Kong, four years in Kenya, and pastorates at Central Tabernacle in Edmonton and Lakeshore Evangelical Church in Montreal. He arrived at Abbotsford in December 1982.

Calvin told us, "I suppose if you were to ask the people here what's important to me, they'd say, 'What he's doing right here.' I can live with that. The reality of pastoring the church is pulling all the strands together to make evangelism and outreach a reality."

If that's the case, Calvin is weaving a tapestry to match the grandeur of his setting.

Frank Tillapaugh

Breaking down the walls of the "fortress church" and transforming it into "the church unleashed" has been the focus of Frank Tillapaugh's nearly twenty years of ministry at Bear Valley Baptist Church in Denver, Colorado.

Since 1972, when he arrived at the struggling congregation, the church has grown from approximately seventy to more than twelve hundred. Amazingly, throughout its growth period, the church continued to meet in a sanctuary that seats 275. The limited facility helped spawn a creative approach to ministry, and Bear Valley has become known for its imaginative and entrepreneurial approach to outreach.

Through the ministry of The Navigators, Frank became a Christian in Germany while serving in the army. Eventually he attended Long Beach State University and Denver Seminary.

Frank describes his formative experiences: "For the first seven years of my Christian life, I served the Lord primarily outside a local-church context. During seminary, two courses turned me on to the local church. First, church history gave me a perspective on where the church has been. I saw a tremendous flexibility. The church has been able to function — sometimes gloriously and other times less than gloriously — in virtually every type of culture for two thousand years.

"The second course was systematic theology. Through studying Scripture and theology, I saw the magnificence of the Body. I had to rethink my parachurch experience. Yes, the parachurch is effective because it specializes, but it pays a high price. That effectiveness has an intended narrowness built in. If a ministry is geared to teens, that's great while they're teens, but someday we all turn twenty. If a ministry is geared to street people, what happens when they go straight?"

This desire to minister to all kinds of people, through all the stages of life, led Frank to emphasize "target group" ministry within the context of the church.

His mentor and former professor, Vernon Grounds, describes Frank: "I must honestly say that in seminary he was not much of a bookworm! I must also say that he is not a scintillating pulpiteer. Neither is he a high-powered salesman nor an adroit administrator. No, Frank is a man who has a passion to be an agent of the Holy Spirit in unleashing the potential of God's people. He has the courage to be unconventional and experimental. He has the gift of infecting others with his own dynamic concept of what Christianity is all about."

Frank brings this innovative and energetic spirit to each of his chapters in this book.

Mastering Outreach and Evangelism

No one ever masters the tasks of outreach and evangelism, of course, as these men will be the first to admit. But few of us are exempt from learning more. And learning more is what this series is about.

As I mentioned, after laying the initial groundwork, these pastors discuss both the structures and the strategies they've employed in their church's mission. Naturally, just as outreach and evangelism often overlap, so do the structures and strategies for doing it. Sometimes a structure becomes a strategy and vice versa. Fire, as Emil Brunner implied, has a passion and power that is not easily contained.

Our outline, then, is not meant to be a neat and systematic explanation of the task. Although we hope this volume will help you more effectively organize your mission, we also trust it will ignite within you the fire to do it better.

— Mark Galli
associate editor, LEADERSHIP
Carol Stream, Illinois

PART ONE

Preparing the Way

I want to integrate evangelism into every hour of the week, so that Christ is carried into people's lives, into our work, play, and socializing.

— Myron Augsburger

CHAPTER ONE

Overcoming the Obstacles to Evangelism

Evangelism is everything we do to make faith in Christ an option. It includes sharing the good word and doing the good deed. But sometimes our words and deeds do not touch the hearts of those we seek to reach. Sometimes obstacles we don't understand hinder our evangelistic efforts.

Some time ago we invited a couple to our home for dinner. He's a member of our church; she isn't. They accepted, but she was so anxious about coming to our home, both because we were white (and they were black) and because we were "religious," that she called several times to change the arrangements. Finally she phoned the afternoon of our engagement and told my wife, Esther, "Don't have a dinner, just a snack. We'll have eaten." So Esther complied and prepared finger food.

They arrived together, but he had come straight from work; he did not know his wife had made the change, and had not eaten dinner. Naturally, he finished several plates of finger food and dessert. Nonetheless, we enjoyed a pleasant evening together. As they were leaving, this woman turned to Esther and said, "Next time we'll come for dinner. I won't be afraid."

Differences in race, culture, education, habits, and social customs had become obstacles between us. That evening, we cleared away a few.

Many things hinder evangelism. Often, our secular, materialistic, individualistic culture gets in the way. Sometimes it's our own insensitivity to other people and subcultures that obstructs the Good News. Fortunately, some Christians are doing brilliant cultural analysis to alert us to such hindrances and suggest how we might overcome them.

Yet there are other obstacles still, stumbling blocks more subtle that we often miss. In my ministry, I've run into them, as have most pastors. Below are listed a few our congregation has had to address. For each obstacle, let me explain how we try to make straight and smooth the way for evangelism.

Obstacle 1: Lack of Trust

Esther and I live in the inner city of Washington, D.C., on the border of a poor neighborhood. Many people here are trapped. Seldom do people leave the ghetto to shop, play, or do business. Consequently, they don't believe that suburbanites, who commute each day into the city but then leave in the evening, understand them. Nor would they trust anyone who would try to minister to them who didn't share their life.

Consequently, when we came to the inner city, we decided to live in a row house in the neighborhood where the church building stands. We relate to our neighbors daily. I'm known as "Rev" in my community, and whether people are churchgoers or not, I spend time with them — sometimes by simply passing the time of day.

A while back, one of my neighbors died while I was out of town. The family of the deceased asked if I would conduct the funeral. Even though I wasn't going to be back for five days, they chose to wait for my return. Why? Because I lived in the neighborhood and they knew me. In the family's words, I was "the only pastor that Dad knew."

Trust, of course, is not just an inner-city issue. Regardless of location, if we want to reach people, we need to build rapport and establish trust, which usually means we must live in the community to which we will minister, whether that means the country or suburbia.

Building trust takes time. Many of my neighbors have lived in the same community all of their lives. Leaving a congregation without reasonable cause suggests to them that our desire to serve may be less than authentic. After eight years of ministry here, I've learned that maintaining a steady presence among people demonstrates genuine care and commitment. After I had ministered several years in the community, one man said to me, "Myron, I've watched you long enough. I've learned I can trust you. I'd like to join your church."

Obstacle 2: Compartmental Evangelism

Some people assume that evangelism is a church-sponsored program that prescribes particular verbal formulas to be delivered at certain times. Inadvertently, perhaps, they compartmentalize life into times of evangelism — one or two hours on a weekday evening — and times for other things.

I am not suggesting that such evangelism is wrong or does not bear fruit. But my experience has taught me not to think of evangelism as a special program. Instead, I want to integrate evangelism into every hour of the week so that Christ is carried into people's lives, into our work, play, and socializing. Even people's finances become our concern.

The poor in the inner city often lack credit references. Most of them, in fact, do not have bank accounts. Cash and food stamps are a way of life for many. Unfortunately, some unscrupulous businesses feed upon this ignorance. Individuals, for instance, may purchase a television set on credit and end up paying for it three times before their payments end.

Our church wanted to deal creatively with this problem. So, with a local credit union, we arranged a way to assist low-income families. Now when people come to the church asking for financial help (to prevent being evicted, for example) we confidentially help them secure a loan with the credit union. This has taught people how to manage money better and helped them establish credit ratings. And as we meet a concrete need, the love of Christ is being shared.

Integrating evangelism with the rest of life causes people to notice the church. Many new Christians in our congregation have told me their interest in becoming a Christian stemmed from their relationship with church members. These were relationships developed outside of regular church-sponsored activities. One young lady said she had been away from the church since her youth. But as she saw the joy of our congregation, she was prompted to visit and discover its source.

This in no way minimizes the need to tell others about sin, forgiveness, and salvation. The deed of love is not enough to express fully the gospel of Christ. But neither is a verbal expression of the gospel effective without the demonstration of love. Evangelism is not a sudden foray into the world with the aim of winning someone, only to retreat just as quickly to a safe haven. It must involve authentic, ongoing relationships with people. It must be integrated with their lives.

Obstacle 3: We'll Do It Our Way

Sometimes a church will discover a particular way to share the love of Christ effectively, and stick with it over the years, even when they could try other things profitably. We ought to be zealous for Christ as we minister in particular ways, through a church food pantry or learning center, for example. These days, I believe, a church mustn't limit itself to one or two expressions of service to the community. Effective outreach to every generation and each sub-culture demands unique approaches. Christ's love takes a variety of forms, some unexpected.

Encouraging the church to keep expanding its service is no easy challenge. But in addition to encouraging teamwork and mutual respect among our people, we affirm each individual's gifts and calling, especially as we grow and change.

For example, a church member serving on our church's stewardship commission was recruited to help a family in our neighborhood find housing. He had been offering his talents in finance and accounting to the congregation. But he discovered that he also could help people find housing. Suddenly, his faith was being expressed in another manner, and he was bringing the love of Christ to needy people.

At the close of worship, we frequently provide "windows of service" when people active in various ministries can share and appeal for help. This not only urges people to find opportunities to express the love of Christ in the community, it also reminds them that there are many ways of doing so.

Obstacle 4: The Anonymous Pastor

Many times, I've deliberately hidden my profession behind other roles. I don't let people know I am a pastor; some people are guarded when around a minister. On some occasions, then, I believe I can better evangelize if people don't know that.

However, in other settings, I take a different stance. I also know that, according to Scripture, Christians are to view themselves as confident ambassadors for Christ. Ambassadors publicly represent their sovereign wherever they live.

An ambassador doesn't enter a community and anonymously reach down the social scale. Nor does he sneak around incognito. Rather, when he enters the country to which he's sent, he offers his credentials to the highest authority present. From that vantage he moves about, working with a variety of people.

When I moved to Washington, D.C., I wanted first to discover and meet respected leaders in the community. I "presented my credentials" to other key pastors and community officials. I told them the purpose of our church's ministry. I also began meeting regularly with an individual who worked for the mayor. I wanted to be sure I came face to face with the leadership of the community — with those who make things happen. Then, whenever people would ask one of these leaders, "What's going on in that church over there?" he could answer. We didn't have to justify our existence or blow our own horn; other people spoke for us.

An additional benefit of meeting these leaders is the insight we gain into the community. For example, early on I said to two black leaders, "Look, I'll make plenty of mistakes, but you can help me avoid a lot of them if you'll let me see the city through your eyes." Among other things, they told me to discover and meet people's actual needs. We should serve people where they need to be served, they said, and not where we prefer to serve. That is wisdom I still try to heed.

Obstacle 5: Denominational Distinctives

I am deeply committed to the Mennonite Anabaptist tradition. However, when my wife and I came to Washington, D.C., although we wanted our congregation to be affiliated with the Mennonite Church, we also wanted it to be multi-denominational in character. The aim of our church, then, is to incorporate individuals from various backgrounds *and* to sustain their distinct identities within our church body.

This approach seems essential in today's world, whether ministry is in an urban, suburban, or rural context. It is unreasonable to expect every individual to change his denominational theology because he wants to participate in a neighborhood church and join an authentic Christian community.

Consequently, our church has adopted a ten-point membership covenant, which is the basis of our life together. The covenant holds us in unity and gives members freedom to practice their faith with diversity.

Take, for example, baptism. We believe the mode of baptism is only a symbol of the reality of one's commitment to Christ. If one person wishes to be baptized by immersion, we perform it that way. If another wants to be baptized by pouring, we baptize him by pouring.

Another example: liturgies for infants. As an Anabaptist congregation, we dedicate infants. But we honor people who believe their child should be baptized. On one occasion, a couple committed to covenant theology wanted their infant baptized. They volunteered to have the sacrament performed elsewhere, knowing infant baptism was not part of the Anabaptist tradition. But the congregation began raising questions. This couple was part of our fellowship, after all. We wanted to surround this couple with Christian love at this important moment in their lives.

After deliberation, we resolved the dilemma by inviting a neighboring Presbyterian minister to baptize the infant at the conclusion of a service. The congregation affirmed its support for this couple as they began the process of raising their child in the knowledge of Christ.

In our multi-denominational congregation, we have members who join to become Mennonites, but we also have Presbyterians, Methodists, Episcopalians, and Evangelical Free, among others, who will remain loyal to their denominational heritage even after they join our church.

When the Obstacles Are Down

Poverty — the kind typically connected with the inner city — was the only condition one family in Washington, D.C., had known. They lived in a basement. They used two couches for beds. A hose, which supplied bathroom water, dangled through a window. An old washtub was placed near a wall as a sink. They had no income.

A church member noticed their plight and told us about them. The mother was willing to work, but had trouble finding employment. Our church tried to address both forms of poverty — the physical and the spiritual. My wife began by finding the mother a job cleaning houses and helping the children find yard work.

After six years of encouragement, friendship, and sharing the gospel, we rejoice in how that family situation has changed. They now live in a rented house that our congregation located for them. One of the children is a senior in a Christian high school, and another now a freshman. The mother continues with her house cleaning and through her earnings is able to provide for the family's physical necessities. (Unfortunately, the father continues to be unproductive and is a continuing concern to us.) In addition, the mother and children play a significant role in the life of our congregation. In this case, distrust has melted as love was expressed.

Evangelism for us isn't relegated to a time slot, nor to one or two types of activities. In short, evangelism is practiced as a way of life. It's not surprising, then, that barriers come down, and that people hear and believe the good news of the gospel. As Jesus said, "By this shall all men know that ye are my disciples, if ye have love one to another" (John 13:35, KJV).

To some degree the shepherd looks after the sheep, while the sheep give birth to the lambs. But then again, if evangelism isn't happening in our lives, it probably won't happen much in the church.

— Calvin C. Ratz

The Pastor's Role

P aul told Timothy, "Do the work of an evangelist," and ever since, evangelism has belonged in a pastor's job portfolio. But how exactly do we go about evangelism as pastors?

Some pastors actually do little personal evangelism. They figure they have plenty of pressing tasks just to provide spiritual leadership for the church. Evangelism is something members can do. So they encourage evangelism, but don't necessarily participate in it.

To some degree the shepherd looks after the sheep, while the sheep give birth to the lambs. But then again, if evangelism isn't happening in our lives, it probably won't happen much in the church. So although we're not singlehandedly responsible for the rescue of souls, I believe we've got to be involved.

It's been said, "A student learns what his teacher knows, but a disciple becomes what his master is." My people will not become what I say they should be; they'll become what they see is important in my life. And that's true with evangelism.

People want to be led, to be inspired, to be challenged. Pastors who lead their churches into evangelism do it primarily by example, by modeling, by making evangelism a priority.

Reluctant Models

Yet for various reasons, pastors may shy away from talking about personal experiences. For example, I hesitate to talk about my personal evangelistic activity because sometimes I'm afraid of embarrassing new converts; I don't want to spotlight them until I can see that their conversions have stuck. Many excellent sermon illustrations occupy the pews each Sunday, but I can't use them. It's much the same with evangelism illustrations; I hesitate to dig up a seed to display its growth.

I overcome that hesitancy by telling stories only at the appropriate time and with the necessary permission. For example, I've used the story of one young man who grew up in our church. When I first came to the church, he attended, but sometimes he'd slip out of church and have a beer in the parking lot. I took a liking to this young farmer and enjoyed talking with him. One day I asked him, "When are you going to get married?"

"I can't get married, Pastor," he replied bluntly. "I gotta marry a Christian girl, and I'm not a Christian. So I can't get married until I get saved. And I'm not ready to get saved."

Over the weeks, I shared my faith with him and asked if he wanted to make a commitment. He wasn't ready. But one day over coffee — a day we hadn't been talking about salvation — he said to me, "Okay. I want to get right," and we prayed there. After that, he became deeply involved in the church, and just a few weeks ago, he married a young Christian woman.

I let his story be told when he was baptized, but I let him do the telling. The story was told another time when I interviewed him in a service. On both occasions, then, I was able to model how evangelism was a part of my life while not embarrassing a new Christian.

Why the desire to trumpet my involvement in this man's life? It's because I've learned that modeling is not so much what I do as what I'm *perceived* to be doing.

Let me explain. People don't know what pastors do. Often they think we're doing things we're not actually doing, such as spending the whole day in blissful contemplation of Scripture for hours on end. Conversely, they miss many of the things I actually do. I may be witnessing to many people throughout the week, but if people think I'm doing something else, I'm not modeling evangelism. Somehow I must help them perceive correctly what I am actually doing. It's important to let people know what actually is taking place in my witness. I cannot assume they know.

A second reason we hesitate to talk about our evangelism is because we don't want to seem presumptuous. We know our inadequacies; we're not the evangelists we should be. That can make us feel inadequate as models, and so we shy away from saying, "Follow me, as I follow Christ." It's too intimidating.

But people will follow us whether we admit it or not. It's not a question of "Am I going to be a model?" The question is, "What kind of a model will I be?" I've got to recognize the messages I'm preaching when I'm not in the pulpit.

Even the fact that sometimes I am a poor model of evangelism may be used for good. At times I simply let the congregation know I share many of their experiences and feelings about evangelism.

I'll often talk about times I muffed an opportunity to witness. For instance, I was aboard a flight out of Toronto a few years ago — the same flight that the day before had crashed. As we were about to take off, the lady next to me said, "D-d-did y-you h-h-hear what happened yesterday?" I noticed her hands were white. I reassured her, but I didn't mention God. When I got off the flight, I thought, *Why didn't I share my faith with her?* It was a perfect opportunity, but I never capitalized on it.

I also tell people, "Look, I'm as scared as you are to witness on a one-to-one basis. Behind the pulpit I have plenty of confidence, but when I'm stripped of that security, I'm as vulnerable as anybody else. It's no easier for me to talk to the person in the restaurant or my neighbor than it is for you. I struggle with the same inhibitions."

People can identify with that. Being transparent, being honest, telling the good as well as the bad — this gives more credibility to the successes we share.

Furthermore, as a pastor, some things work against me when I try to witness. Some people think, *He's just a preacher trying to convert me.*

The first time I met the neighbor who lives in back of us, he said, "I understand you're a preacher. I just want you to know I'm the only sinner on the block." He was really saying, "Keep your distance." I later learned another Christian had pursued him obnoxiously. Since I was a pastor, I was automatically suspect.

Ministers have received bad press recently. Therefore, fearing opposition or misunderstanding because of my position, it's easy not to make the effort to witness. I easily become too self-conscious.

Yet, being a pastor can be an advantage. It certainly helps me answer questions more easily. I'm not afraid of what people may ask or the direction a conversation might take. Pastoral training serves me in good stead.

I also have many opportunities to witness. After all, the gospel is my vocation. I get paid to do what most people have to do on the side. Inquirers come to me even if I don't seek them out. People refer friends to me. Christianity comes up in routine social conversations about my occupation. I have ample opportunity to talk about my faith — if I don't let deficient spiritual self-esteem hinder me.

Intentional Modeling

Even though I am sometimes a poor model, I aim to model well. So I practice what I call *intentional modeling* to distinguish what

I want to do from the merely passive, inactive influence I usually have.

What do I want to say with my life about evangelism? That life is short, eternity is long, Jesus can make a difference in it all, and *I'm* responsible for getting that message to others. I want my life to be an example that all these factors are utterly true.

I also want to model that evangelism is enjoyable, not something dreadful and threatening but nonetheless necessary. To do that, I tell stories about the joy of seeing a life transformed by Christ, the gratitude of people who thank us for sharing Christ, and the satisfaction of leading someone to Christ for eternity! Nothing compares to that. And I try to communicate that feeling.

But if I'm going to model that joy intentionally, I have to do five things as a pastor.

First, evangelism must be *a personal priority for me.* If I don't live it, I can't preach it with conviction.

As a pastor, I can wrap myself with activities that deal solely with Christians. So it's easy to justify a lack of time for personal evangelism: I have to write a sermon or visit the saints. There just aren't many evenings left to invite neighbors and friends over.

So, I deliberately place myself in situations in which I can talk to people about Christ. Such situations, by God's grace, arise in the normal flow of the ministry; I just have to learn to take advantage of them.

A while back a young couple came to worship. I noticed them during the service, not merely because they were new, but from their rapt attention — they didn't take their eyes off me when I was preaching. After the service, I met them. We talked briefly, and I asked, "Can we get together sometime?"

"We'd love to," the man said.

I met them that week in a restaurant for lunch. They were searching for something in life, it turned out, but they hadn't found it. We talked about faith, and I asked, "Are you ready to accept Jesus into your lives?"

They looked around and said, "Here?"

"What better place?" I said. So we held hands, and over half-filled coffee cups, they each prayed to receive Christ. Both are now active in the church.

Another opportunity I take advantage of is conversations with newcomers who say, "We used to go to such-and-such church." I used to assume they were Christians, but I've found that often they aren't. People transferring from other communities are prime candidates, if not for evangelism, at least for a challenge to greater discipleship.

2   Second, evangelism must be *a passionate priority*. Passion has to exist — somewhere — for evangelism to work. Paul said, "Christ's love compels us" (2 Cor. 5:14, NIV). I shouldn't pastor a church if I can't demonstrate a passionate care for the lost, because if evangelism doesn't bubble to the surface in my life, how will others catch the vision to evangelize? I need to be appropriately driven to share the gospel.

Third, intentional modeling requires me to get *out of my office*. I prefer to manage church affairs, study, and prepare sermons — activities that keep me in an office with the door closed. But I'm not modeling evangelism if I spend an inordinate amount of time away from people. So I'm learning to get out to work with people.

Tom Peters in *A Passion for Excellence* encourages "management by walking around." He says a manager should be out of his office a third of the time. I'm learning to pastor by walking around.

The benefits are many. "Peoplework" keeps me fresh and makes me visible. When I'm among people, they can *see* my priority for evangelism at work. And getting out puts me in contact with non-Christians.

I plan opportunities to be with people, like after church on Sunday evening. That's a big occasion in our community. And I usually accept invitations to people's homes, because I can interact with several couples in a relaxed atmosphere.

I find that when I catch people off guard in nonreligious settings, I accomplish a great deal evangelistically. Communication studies show that persuasive communication that comes unexpectedly in an unusual environment has more chance of being effective than if it came at a predictable time from a predictable person.

For instance, if I stand up on Sunday morning and say, "You should pray," people yawn and think, *Well, yeah. We know that. He's supposed to say that.* But if I'm having coffee with the guys and I say, "You know, in the last week the Lord's been talking to me about praying more for the people I'm trying to bring to the Lord," it's powerful.

Some pastors need to be pushed into the study. But I'm the type who needs to get outside the walls of my office to model and practice among others the evangelistic priorities I hold dear.

Fourth, *the method must have integrity* if my intentional modeling is to be effective. If I go to the Bible for what I believe, I shouldn't look only to the world for methodology. I'm not against using technology and any other appropriate modern means to spread the gospel, but I also want to be sure to build evangelism on the foundation of love rather than gimmicks.

I could attract a crowd with a Christian cowboy riding an appaloosa pony across the platform, but that is hardly a biblical model of evangelism. I don't want to sacrifice the integrity of the gospel for the sake of pulling a crowd, or compromise the message in order to make the gospel more palatable.

For example, although we have a strong music program, I refuse to build the church around music. We will grow our own music ministry, but we won't import one. Certainly we will supplement our ministry at times, but we're not going to build our outreach on a string of big names and events just to attract the outsider. It is our church, our people, our program that must attract and hold people's attention for the gospel to do its work.

Our evangelistic methods should lead people to repentance and faith and a decision to follow Jesus Christ, not just to attend church programs. The church has to be built on biblical principle, and so does the evangelism I model.

Finally, effective intentional modeling requires that I *pray about evangelism*. This obvious point sometimes gets overlooked. So I try not only to talk prayer, but to do it.

More specifically, I pray for an increase of harvesters. I don't have to pray for the harvest; it's there. But the harvesters are few, so they get my prayers. I pray that evangelism will happen through the people of my church.

Personally, I also pray for passion for the lost, for opportunities and courage and faith to grab the opportunities as they come. As I've mentioned, I'm reluctant and sometimes discouraged. A friend of mine was distributing food in Ethiopia, and while there he talked to some nuns who did similar work. He asked them, "How do you handle the devastation and the hurt and agony you see day after day?"

One nun replied, "Prayer. If we do not have God in our hearts, nothing else works." Likewise, only if I have God in my heart will evangelism "work."

Modeling the Message

Over the years, I've learned a difficult lesson: I must not only speak about and model evangelism, I must also model the Good News in my life. Evangelism is not just a technique, but a way of Christian living.

A friend of mine, a public relations officer for a major corporation, was a Christian, but he was living out his faith rather casually. Then he was asked to present a lecture on public relations. He was driving home the point that successful public relations depends on matching a product's quality with the image the company projects about the product. He talked about going into a large department store that had advertised its friendly, courteous service. But he was treated terribly. The reality didn't match the image, and the disparity between the public-relations spiel and reality made him angry. But he discovered an application beyond mere public relations.

"Going home from that store," he told me later, "it was as if the Lord said to me, 'That's your life. You're modeling one thing in church in front of people, but your kids see the reality — and the discrepancy — at home. The product *you're* advertising is not matched by the reality.' I realized that what I show on Sunday has to be backed up by reality. It can't be phony. Maybe I can get by with a little hype the first couple of years, but soon people see it for what it is. The reality is, I've got to produce what I claim to have."

When it comes to Christian living, none of us will ever be able to model all we should, nor will everything we do come out looking the way we intend. But intentional modeling of evangelism means that the life I live must bear some resemblance to the message I preach.

It's up to us to set the ideal by the way we talk to people, the tone of voice, the vocabulary we use, the examples we choose, the vulnerability we allow. By these means we can say to our congregations, "Folks, this is what evangelism means. I'm not perfect at it; you're not perfect. But let's go on a pilgrimage together. Let's share the love of Christ with our friends and neighbors, near and far."

Modeling Comes Full Circle

The eyes of fellow staff members, church leaders, and church members watch my actions and note my words. But after many years of modeling, I've begun to notice their actions and words.

For some time, for example, I've tried to imprint upon my staff the values and emphases I consider important — evangelism being foremost. I've wanted to inspire them as evangelists, not just as managers of programs or departments.

So, as a staff we've talked often about evangelism. I've made sure it's a regular agenda item. I've also tried to spend much time with my staff, so that in casual conversations staff members pick up what's important to me.

And I'm starting to see modeling pay off. One of our staff came up with the idea of having a hamburger stand at the local fair. So we put up a tent, cooked hamburgers, and played Christian music nonstop for four days there. That gave us visibility in the community, and the people who were involved ended up getting great training as counselors and hosts and hostesses.

The idea for this activity began when that man — who wasn't particularly responsible for evangelism in our church — said, "Let's do something to reach out to the people of our community." Such ideas now surface regularly at staff meetings.

I've seen the same thing happen with our board. As with all

boards, ours faces the tensions of balancing the budget, meeting congregational needs, and setting priorities. Naturally, the priority I regularly encourage them to pursue and budget for is evangelism.

Apparently, it's taken effect. I've noticed recently that any time I take to the board a proposal with a legitimate evangelistic twist to it, they'll go with it. While the board has held a tight rein on expenditures during our recent building program, they haven't hesitated to spend money on items with an evangelistic payoff. They quickly paid for ten of us to travel 450 miles to a two-day conference on church evangelism. They eagerly footed the bill for an evangelistic luncheon geared to unchurched widows, which eighty-five ladies attended. They gladly agreed to pay for two evangelistic banquets: one directed to the construction workers for our new building, and another for 150 unchurched community leaders.

And although our board is not afraid to let a dated church program die, if the program has evangelistic possibilities, they hesitate, saying, "Hey, evangelism is our lifeblood. Let's rework the program and revitalize it if possible."

To put it another way, my staff and board now are prodding *me* to make the church and its ministries more seeker friendly. They're evaluating my preaching and schedule to help me be a more evangelistic pastor. They are producing ideas for outreach, novel methods for reaching outsiders, and ways to make our services sensitive to those who are not believers.

Last week, my staff initiated a discussion on how I could improve my preaching to better tune in to today's unchurched, secular mind. They initiated a lengthy discussion on reformatting our services to strip them of in-house vocabulary and practices that make it difficult for outsiders to accept or understand the gospel.

It's when my staff and board start pushing me that I know my staff has caught the passion for evangelism that I feel in my heart.

PART TWO
Structures

Positioning a church for evangelism goes far beyond implementing a program or hiring additional staff. Ultimately, it takes a corporate change of heart.

— Calvin C. Ratz

CHAPTER THREE

Structuring a Church for Active Evangelism

An ad by the Canadian investment firm *Nesbitt Thompson* featured this line: "Anyone can ride a bull, but it takes discipline to dance with a bear."

That's true, as any investor knows. When a "bull market" is surging ahead, as it was through the early 1980s, everyone makes money. But when it's a declining "bear market," that's not the case.

Pastoring has its equivalent. A friend, who'd never experienced significant growth in any of the churches he'd pastored, has suddenly enjoyed a spurt of numerical growth. "I'm not doing anything different," he claims, "but all of a sudden our congregation is expanding rapidly." That pastor is riding a bull market.

The fact is, several other churches in his community are experiencing similar growth. The demographics of his community, the subculture of his congregation, and an influx of transferees have all coalesced to nearly double his congregation in a couple of years. It has revitalized his church.

Many of us, however, are in a bear market. We work hard for every convert. We struggle to maintain our gains. It takes discipline to dance with a bear — the discipline of developing a long-range strategy and a balanced philosophy of ministry, the discipline of rejecting passing fads and apparent quick fixes, the discipline of developing personal character and integrity.

I began at my present church just over seven years ago. For the most part, I've danced with a bear. Growth has been neither automatic nor easy. In the process, I've had to come to grips with my own approach to ministry. I've had to discover how to direct the church's spiritual energy toward evangelism, when for years it's been comfortable with the status quo.

One Sunday morning, shortly after arriving, I asked the congregation of about six hundred how many of them had been converted to Christ in the previous two years. I was trying to excite the people about what God was doing. Just six hands went up. Obviously, any growth had been transfer growth.

That brought my job into sharp focus: I had to move the congregation beyond its proud history to the point of wanting evangelism and making it happen. Since then, I've discovered the frustrations and joys of seeing a well-established church come to grips with its mission.

There's no three-step, money-back-guaranteed approach to positioning a church for evangelism. Rather, I've discovered it's an ongoing process of personal growth and evaluation, coupled with sensitivity to the history and needs of the congregation.

Looking back, here's what I've discovered is important for those wanting to create an environment in which evangelism flourishes.

Establish the Church's Vision

A church, if it expects to rouse from lethargy, must know why it exists and what God expects it to accomplish. This means going beyond knowing that it's God's intention for all churches to evangelize. A church must discover God's plan for *its* particular contribution to the kingdom. Some congregations are called to be spiritual hospitals, some social activists, some teaching centers. Still others are front-line attack forces.

The first thing I had to know was my own convictions. What specifically does God want to happen in my church, and how? Further, it wasn't enough to have a solo vision for the church; key leaders needed to share the conviction.

So discovering God's will for our church became a mutual quest. It all came together at a pastor-board retreat about a year after my arrival. There, following prior reading in evangelism and church growth, we sought the direction God wanted our church to head.

We asked two questions at the retreat: First, what should be the direction of the church? Second, how best can we reach our community with the gospel? I well remember the discussion. One man said, "We've got to get off the church parking lot and out into the traffic."

Another observed, "We're growing through transfer growth, not conversion growth. We've got to do something about the apathy people have for the lost. And, Pastor, I need a new passion as much as anyone!"

After considerable discussion and prayer, the board was unanimous: We were committed to growth, which meant constructing a larger sanctuary. In addition, we outlined twenty basic principles to follow in reaching these goals, such things as prayer, an emphasis on Scripture, an appeal to the unchurched, and strong pastoral leadership.

These principles were more than vague notions; we specifically described them. For example, we recognized that growing churches had one dominant preacher, rather than a rotating team. Consequently, I was asked to commit myself to the bulk of the preaching. I didn't enjoy cutting back the staff's pulpit access, but it was an action we felt we had to do to make an impact on the unchurched.

To be honest, a great deal of optimism pervaded the gathering, almost to the point of being unrealistic. But in retrospect, the euphoria was necessary and God-given. It provided the impetus to get us moving and face what was ahead.

After the retreat, we summarized our convictions on paper. Each succeeding year, we've hauled out that document to check our progress. There's little we'd change today. It still outlines our basic convictions concerning where we should be going and how we feel God wants us to get there.

Excite the Congregation with the Vision

When a pastor blows the trumpet for evangelism, it can scare the congregation as much as excite it. The call to evangelism is first of all a call for change, and change can be threatening. So care is needed to woo the congregation toward evangelism.

Our pastor-board discussions brought unanimity, faith, and excitement. But we held the information to ourselves, proceeding slowly because we knew the importance of building confidence and trust. I was still new. Sheep won't follow the voice of a strange shepherd.

Given my choice, I would have loved to proceed as quickly as possible to build the new sanctuary. But in rousing the congregation to fulfill its mission, I didn't want to divide the church. Spiritual growth had to take place before there could be effective evangelism. Since we believed a healthy body would grow, we tried to go slowly.

Circumstances, however, forced us to go public with our vision more quickly than we had planned. Within weeks after our retreat, property adjoining the present church suddenly became available. We would either buy the additional five acres immediately to provide for expansion or we would forfeit the opportunity. But to buy the land would signal to the unprepared congregation our intent to grow. The land acquisition became the test of whether the congregation had the will for evangelism.

Our problem was that many in the congregation had been conditioned previously to think the church would handle growth through starting another congregation. It wasn't that people had evangelistic vision; they just wanted to transfer growth elsewhere and maintain a comfortable size. So our expansion plans wouldn't naturally sit easily.

A new vision for a church can be both thrilling and traumatic for the congregation. For those who buy the vision, it's exhilarating; for those who are threatened, it can mean fear and confusion. We experienced the gamut.

From the time we learned the land was available, we had just four weeks to complete the deal. We announced the plan, shared our vision, called a congregational vote, and managed to carry the motion. But we weren't able to bring everyone on board. We unsettled some cherished values. We learned that spiritual renewal and revival don't often happen in a business meeting.

Sometimes leaders get so far ahead of their people that they're perceived as the enemy. That's what started to happen to us. We discovered about half the congregation was highly supportive, a quarter vocally negative, and a quarter bewildered. So after purchasing the property, we backed off and gave the congregation time to catch up.

The people had to feel a personal conviction for evangelism. They had to want to touch our community and grow. We used a variety of means to encourage people to fulfill the vision God had given us.

● *The pulpit.* The pulpit can elevate the vision from the secular to the spiritual. So I challenged our people with the needs of our community. I tried to keep the issue not how many people we could get to join our church but how many in our community were lost without Jesus Christ.

I tried to avoid guilt, a poor motivator with only short-term benefits. Its long-term effect is usually cynicism and fear. I did my best to affirm the pioneers by acknowledging that the strength of the church today is a result of their vision and faithful service.

● *Conversations.* Tom Peters, in his book *Thriving on Chaos,* suggests a leader should become the vision's foremost itinerant preacher: "Do not let a single day pass without taking at least two or three opportunities to deliver a three-minute stump speech on the vision." Wanting to be effective, I tried to develop ways to introduce our vision into most conversations and summarize our dreams.

A couple of questions helped turn conversations toward our vision for evangelism. I'd ask, "What's God been telling you about our church lately?" and "Are you aware of some of the things God is doing in our church?" In the discussion that followed, it wasn't hard to summarize what I believed God was saying to the church and how the collective leadership of the church was responding.

✓   ● *Encouraging ownership of the vision.* One of the deacons tipped me off to a nascent problem: "Pastor, some people think this is just your project. We've got to correct that impression." Apparently some people thought I wanted a larger church to feed my ego. One person called the new sanctuary "the pastor's pet project." Because of this mistaken notion, we devised a program to share the vision yet take the spotlight off me.

We worked through the committees of the church, particularly our leadership council. At several council meetings, we dealt with the question: What will enable us to evangelize our community? We allowed time for free expression of ideas, fears, and concerns. Lay leaders chaired many of these sessions. I wanted others committed to the vision to answer questions to demonstrate I wasn't the only one with the vision for change.

● *Opinion leaders.* We reached out through those we perceived to be congregational opinion leaders. These opinion leaders aren't necessarily the elected officials. They're simply the people who command attention when they speak. Their influence may be felt in a business meeting, but more likely it's felt over coffee after church or in parking lot conversations.

I lunched with many of these opinion leaders to challenge them individually. Most are enthusiastic in their support; a few have remained aloof to the vision.

● *Testimonials.* For about a year, once a month we had some-one share what the church meant to him and how he was praying for the church to reach out to our community. God spoke to the congregation through these testimonials. People began to realize that concern for growth was widespread.

One particularly helpful testimonial came from a man who'd been in the church about three years and who was working in the Sunday school. People heard the passionate concern of someone who wasn't part of the church establishment or even closely associ-ated with me. He described how the Sunday school was growing, how we had several classes meeting in hallways, and how the youth department was meeting in a nearby school.

His words weren't the most polished, but the congregation was moved. We turned a corner that morning.

● *An abundance of information and means.* I asked another pastor what he'd learned going through a similar process. He said, "Give the people more information than you think they need." That was valuable advice.

I learned the dangers of relying solely on verbal announce-ments for key information. The spoken word can be misunderstood and forgotten. In addition, at least 30 percent of most congregations is absent on a given Sunday, so the only sure way to inform all the people is through the mail. Though it's expensive, it's paid good dividends for us to communicate regularly with the congregation through the mail.

The board also circulated the "Facing the Future, Fulfilling Our Mission" document to the congregation. It detailed our goals and methods and outlined our ten-year plan, the projected growth for the community and church, the concepts of our expansion, and also the idea of planting another congregation.

While some folk will never take time to read such material, I learned that those who are slow in accepting a new plan do take time to read. The literature laid the plan out so there could be no misunderstanding.

● *Themes and emphases.* A well-stated theme can mobilize people to a vision. When the theme is visible continually — posters, bulletins, signs, bookmarks — it constantly reminds people of the church's passion.

Each year we've set a theme tied to our overall vision of evangelistic and spiritual growth. We've used phrases such as "Growing Together" and "Building for the Future." We called one year simply "The Year of Evangelism," and during the year taught personal evangelism and programmed several special events, culminating with a Billy Graham–style crusade.

Gradually the vision has spread.

Reshape the Ministries

As a vision for evangelism begins to grow, new challenges emerge. First, it becomes obvious that *many of the church programs are introverted.*

We're probably typical; most of our programs were geared to meet the needs of our people rather than touch those in the community. Our research indicated 95 percent of our ministries had little or no evangelistic focus.

For example, our Crusader program, a midweek activity for boys and girls, had plenty of children but no evangelistic component. In fact, the setup made it next to impossible for an outsider to join. The program not only didn't evangelize; it was a barrier to growth.

We've since infused leadership with a heart for those outside the church. We've worked to make the program more porous, allowing newcomers a gracious and welcome way in. Now we're aggressively looking for ways to bring in unchurched children.

All churches face the same pressures. The need to provide support and encouragement to existing Christians is legitimate, but it's not spiritual harvesting. Growing churches find ways to build an evangelistic component into all their programs; they also establish programs that have evangelism as a primary purpose.

Second, there's *a need to realign the personnel in the church's programs.* Those with both a heart and an aptitude for evangelism can be shifted into positions where their gifts reap the maximum benefits.

We discovered, for example, that the secretary for our music department, a woman who spent hours each week arranging music books and supplies for our choirs, was gifted in sharing her faith. But she was buried in a church office, cut off from the people to whom she could witness. We've since redeployed her; she's leading our neighborhood Bible studies and helping in our counseling ministries.

Not all department leaders live comfortably with the implications of the new emphasis on evangelism. Some find it threatening. Some of our solid workers felt good working among Christians but were intimidated by the thought of working with non-Christians. So we lost a few. But we try to help them find less threatening but equally important ministries.

Third, as a vision for evangelism takes hold, it becomes clear that *a church has to rethink its target audience.* It has to look outside its four walls to identify the groups it is most capable of reaching.

To be realistic, not only is our community unlikely to become fully evangelized, but also our church doesn't have the capacity to reach everyone. So, without playing God, we've tried to identify those groups most apt to respond positively to the gospel in our setting. This enables us to target their needs and maximize the use of our workers. We've identified four groups we're most likely to reach:

• *The hurting.* Naaman came to God at a time of crisis. Jesus attracted the diseased, the deluded, and the depressed. He appealed to the ostracized and the social misfits. It's the same today; people in need are prime candidates for responding to the gospel.

The gospel has always appealed to those in the lower half of society. The trouble is, most of our people have been saved for several years. God has blessed them in the interval, and now they're socially and economically removed from the most responsive segment of society. Yuppies and dinks (double income, no kids) don't relate well with people on welfare.

We've tried to take this into consideration in planning for evangelism. Our youth, for example, run a monthly event called

Sonshine Coffee House that is geared to the mentally and physically handicapped. It's thrilling to watch our kids reading a story to a blind child or playing games with someone in a wheelchair.

• *Young adults.* Several consultants have indicated that churches usually grow in the 18–35 age bracket in which people are making major choices and establishing family lifestyles. So we've set up three age-grouped programs with these people, to reach out, to integrate them into the church, and to provide teaching and pastoral care.

We've tried to make singles feel welcome, not by segregating them (though we do have a singles class) but by integrating them into the life of the church. Each of our adult fellowship groups has a single adult on its committee.

Our monthly Ladies' Night Out program looks to those outside the church. The evening provides instruction in such things as microwave cooking and Christmas wrapping but concludes with a brief explanation of the Christian faith. Currently about half those attending come from outside the church.

• *The over-55 crowd.* We're discovering seniors are responsive to the gospel. I've baptized several in their 80s.

Our city has twice the number of seniors as the national average, so we're programming to meet their needs with a monthly luncheon and a Wednesday program of table games and carpet bowling. In addition, our seniors' choir sings at least one Sunday a month, performs cantatas, and appears regularly at community events. We have a seniors' handbell choir, a seniors' orchestra, and a men's octet called "The Singing Grampas." These people have time and talent to devote to the church. We just need to reach out to them.

• *Children.* Children are still the segment of society most responsive to the gospel. We've divided this potential harvest into two groups: children of church families and those from non-Christian homes.

We've seriously investigated our success rate at keeping our own children. Biological evangelism doesn't happen automatically. To meet the need, we hold children's crusades, and we're reemphasizing Sunday school and several midweek activities.

One of our pastors has established an informal group for parents of older teens and young adults who aren't living for God. He meets with these parents, helps them deal with their sense of failure, and helps them find ways to reach their grown children.

Upgrade Platform Ministries

What happens on the platform is critical because it touches newcomers and influences people on the fringe. Consequently, we've worked to upgrade our Sunday-worship effectiveness.

We don't want to be so concerned about keeping the Christians happy that we make outsiders feel uncomfortable. Twenty-five years ago, 88 percent of Canadian university students said it was important to have a philosophy of life. A recent survey indicated that number has dropped to 39 today. People obviously have changed. The truth is, if we're presenting the gospel the same way we did ten years ago, we're probably missing the mark today. To hit the mark, we've worked out several goals.

● *We will make church a positive experience for outsiders.* Ours is an experience-oriented generation, not a thinking generation, and our churches have felt the shift. Those entering a church sanctuary today are more interested in feeling good spiritually than in gaining biblical knowledge. Inspiration has replaced information as the hot button in today's church market.

This presents us with a dilemma, because religious experience without biblical knowledge fosters fanaticism and confusion. Fortunately, authentic, biblical Christianity does provide an experience. In the New Testament, both the gathering of believers and the public proclamation of the gospel to outsiders were intense, heart-moving encounters. People experienced relationship and emotion. There was joy, anger, conviction, sorrow, and tension. Everyone who touched New Testament Christians experienced something.

We want people to have a legitimate experience that brings them closer to both God and their friends. We may offer this experience through warm interaction in the foyer, the tasteful use of humor, soaring music, or a well-developed illustration that touches the emotions. We want all our services to lead to an encounter with Almighty God — the most heart-stopping, life-changing experience possible.

• *We will provide a warm, relaxed atmosphere.* I used to be all business on the platform, but now I've concluded every church needs a Willard Scott, the weatherman on NBC's "Today" show who daily mentions some Boy Scout in Kansas or wishes happy birthday to some 101-year-old lady in Idaho. He's a "people person" who creates a warm, caring atmosphere. We need more of that. No matter the size of the congregation, real people are important, and they're interested in other real people.

Obviously the atmosphere of the service ought to usher people into the presence of God. But how does that happen? Today, more than ever, people respond to a relaxed atmosphere. People don't want to come to church to be lectured, and they certainly won't bring a guest to a setting that's strained, heavy, or eccentric.

I've always striven for dignity in a service, but sometimes in achieving dignity, I've sacrificed the relaxed atmosphere people need. We're working at closing the emotional distance between pulpit and pew. I often take time to chat with the people, although I try to keep it separate from the sermon. A friend of mine calls it "pastoring from the pulpit." I want to be transparent, to let people see that those on the platform are essentially no different from those in the pew.

• *We will waste no time.* It's amazing how easily worship time is wasted. Radio and television preachers know the danger of dead spots. The fact is, dead time hurts any service by inviting thoughts to wander. Here are some things we've done to honor the time of member and visitor alike:

— Eliminated 95 percent of verbal announcements. They're in the bulletin, and that's it. Interestingly, it hasn't affected attendance at activities. Verbal announcements impress department leaders, but few others.

— Eliminated introductions of musical groups. The information is listed in the bulletin. Musicians are trained to be in place at the appropriate moment, so time isn't lost while they're walking to the platform.

— Tripled the number of offering bags used by the ushers. That cut four minutes from the time it took to collect the offering.

— Rearranged the logistics of serving Communion, saving about ten minutes in the Communion service.

● *Preaching will relate to life.* I've heard preaching called "the fine art of talking in someone else's sleep." Regrettably, I must plead guilty to putting more than one person to sleep on Sunday morning, and when I have, it's usually because I haven't been touching people where they live. Every Sunday, I have to earn my credentials, my right to speak. Paul told Titus, "Make the teaching about God our Savior attractive" (Titus 2:10).

If a church is to be evangelistic, the people in the pew have to feel the preacher understands them and knows what's going on in today's world. Illustrations have to be current. Facts must be accurate, statements substantiated. We're not called to be pop psychologists, but we *are* called to lift up Jesus Christ in such a way that people recognize him as the solution to their frustrations, hurts, and despair.

I'm working on both the style and content of my preaching now more than ever before. I've developed four checks for my sermons that help me stay on track. First, I plan my invitation prior to writing the final draft. Every sermon is designed to get a response. Second, I try to write my sermon concept in seventeen words or less. If I can't, my sermon doesn't have focus, and I probably don't know what I'm talking about. Third, I write a description of one person I'm trying to reach and ask myself, *Will this person relate to what I'm trying to say?* Fourth, I ask myself, *Will a non-Christian understand the language I'm using?*

● *We will provide special events and services especially for outsiders.* People don't want to bring a neighbor the morning the pastor speaks on stewardship. They want to know when it's a good time to bring their friends to church. So we try to provide special events and services, and tell the people that these services are designed with outsiders in mind.

Recently several of our Sunday evening services dealt with

age groupings: for seniors, "When I'm Old and Gray;" for young adults, "The Generic Generation;" and for those in between, "Handling the Middle Ages." Other evenings hit contemporary issues, family life, and practical ways of coping with life. Drama has proved an effective way to explain the gospel to non-Christians, so we do three or four productions a year.

When the conduct of our services doesn't go smoothly, it tells visitors, "This group doesn't have their act together. They don't care enough to look after the details." And, sadder yet, it's a statement to outsiders that Jesus doesn't relate to today's world. That's the message we don't want to communicate; that's the idea we fight through a concerted effort to upgrade our platform ministries.

People like Bill make the effort worthwhile. For a couple of years, Bill kept telling me about Dave, a man he worked with as a mechanic in a maintenance shop. Bill asked me to pray that God would help him as he witnessed to Dave. One day, Dave responded to Bill and to the Lord and accepted Christ. Bill continued to work with Dave and helped lead him to spiritual maturity. Today Dave is fully integrated into our church and is, in turn, reproducing his faith in the lives of others. That's the kind of church I want us to be.

Positioning a church for ongoing evangelism goes far beyond implementing a program or hiring additional staff. Ultimately, it takes a corporate change of heart.

Pastors can engender that attitude, but only the Holy Spirit can bring about an intense passion for spiritual harvesting. Dancing with a bear can be terrifying, but if the Holy Spirit is orchestrating the music, it will be life-changing and fulfilling.

Too often we take our most committed people and make them rear-echelon bureaucrats instead of front-line officers. We produce managers, not ministers. We need to streamline our structures, freeing our leaders to be primarily ministers, not managers.

— Frank Tillapaugh

CHAPTER FOUR

Giving an Ingrown Church an Outward Focus

After a year of following Jesus Christ and being trained by parachurch organizations, my wife and I could have been told, "There is an apartment complex; move in and start a *ministry*." And we would have understood: move in, meet people, present the gospel in a variety of ways, and perhaps hold a Bible study in our apartment.

Later, when I became a pastor, I found not everyone shared that understanding. If I suggested to church people, "Let's have a ministry in that apartment complex," they'd return a blank stare.

They didn't reject the idea; they simply couldn't comprehend it. Terms like *apartment complex, military base, college campus* and the word *ministry* simply didn't fit together. Ministry meant passing out bulletins, serving on committees, teaching Sunday school, and singing in the choir.

In short, ministry had little to do with reaching people beyond our walls. Ministry meant serving the people inside.

When I came to Bear Valley Baptist Church seventeen years ago, there were some good reasons for that. The church had gone through five pastors in the previous seven years. The congregation (attendance: forty) hadn't made a payment on their building in two years. With all that going on, no one had the time, energy, or inclination to think about reaching people in the community; the focus was survival.

Before I came, for example, most of one business meeting was spent debating the merits of fixing the broken typewriter in the church office. They finally decided the church didn't have the money to repair it, but a member who lived near the church owned a typewriter, so, the members reasoned, if the pastor needed one, he could walk down two or three doors and ask to use it.

We soon learned our church's focus on internal matters wasn't that unusual. Ever since, I've struggled, prayed, and studied to answer: What does it take to get a church to reach out to the community? How can we move beyond the "fortress mind-set"?

To my joy, over those seventeen years I've seen our church develop an outward focus. For example, currently we have twenty-five outreach ministries that target unwed mothers, jail inmates, international students, singles, the unchurched elderly, members of cults (and their families), and other groups. Here are some of the principles that have helped give an ingrown church an outward focus.

Bring People Face to Face with the Needs

The first principle in expanding people's vision is: get them to see, up close, the great needs of the people in the community.

This is harder than it sounds, because many churches have

value systems that don't emphasize getting involved in the complex world outside the church. Before World War II, America retained a predominantly rural orientation, so American churches were built upon rural values: stability, harmony, intimacy. During the frontier era, for example, the Methodists and Baptists were tremendously successful in planting churches in rural areas, and the churches later were characterized by these values.

Since World War II, however, America has become increasingly urban and has adopted urban values: change, diversity, accepting conflict (and managing it), bigness, and mobility. Tom Peters, co-author of *In Search of Excellence,* maintains that in today's world we must learn to *Thrive on Chaos* (the title of a subsequent book).

Yet in many cases, the church has clung to traditional understandings that say, in effect, "God's work is to be done in traditional, safe settings," not in the world at large. Consider the burgeoning population of single adults. Over a decade ago we had a typical singles ministry in our church: seven or eight singles, who had been raised in Baptist churches, meeting in a corner of our building. Then I heard Ray Stedman of Peninsula Bible Church say they had baptized seventy-five singles recently. Why? They realized sophisticated San Francisco singles wouldn't come to a church building but would attend a breakfast in a local restaurant. *Of course!* I thought. *Let's move the singles to a local restaurant.*

The original room we rented holds one hundred people, and we filled it and then rented a restaurant in another shopping center. Soon those two groups gave birth to a group that met in a condominium clubhouse. The group of seven or eight has grown to over two hundred.

The rural values of harmony and intimacy and stability remain vital in an urban age, especially within small groups. But to minister effectively to those outside the church, we have to hold these values in balance with the need to reach out. We've found face-to-face apprehension of community needs can open up a tight circle. Let me illustrate three of many ways to help people loosen their grip on fortress thinking.

Some time ago, James Craig of the West Lafayette (Indiana)

Christian Church wrote me about a creative idea: "One November Sunday, with no prior notice to our members (except for a few key personnel), we asked our congregation to grab their coats and head out the door. Chartered city buses carried us through trailer parks, sprawling new subdivisions, apartment complexes, stately old neighborhoods, and student housing. Carefully prepared scripts read by "tour guides" helped us see 100,000 people living in more than 52 apartment complexes, 150 subdivisions, 23 student dormitories, 15 mobile home parks, and 19 nursing homes. Half are unchurched, and informed estimates indicate that five thousand unchurched families in our community are open to enrolling their children in Sunday school, participating in Bible study, or identifying with a local church. What a challenge!"

An Australian pastor told me he took a man from his church to a funeral he was conducting. This member observed unchurched parents grieving the loss of their 12-year-old son. He was so overwhelmed by it that he asked the pastor for a list of all the families for whom the pastor had conducted funerals in the past five years. He invited those families to a grief group. Approximately thirty people attend the bimonthly meeting, and in the first three months, three have prayed to become Christians. There is tremendous power in coming face to face with the need.

I discovered this one week when I preached a message on helping the poor. As part of the message, I mentioned that in Colorado incidents of child abuse rose from 176 reported cases in 1971 to over 10,000 in 1981. "Half of these cases are in our Denver metro area," I said, "and yet the head of Denver Social Services tells me she has only three hundred to four hundred volunteers to help these kids; the other 4,600 abused or neglected children have to be put on a waiting list." At the end of the message, I said, "The invitation for this morning's sermon will be given tomorrow night when the head of Denver Social Services comes to tell us what she's up against."

As a result of that meeting, nearly sixty members of our congregation signed up to help. Dubbed "The Care Company," members of this group meet weekly with abused or neglected children, neglectful parents (mostly single mothers), indigent elderly, and juvenile offenders. The ministry probably never would have begun had not people been brought face to face with the need.

Spotlight Ministers, Not Managers

Another way to encourage people to minister outside the congregation is to highlight church members who do so. Unfortunately, in most churches the spotlight is given to those who manage, not those who minister. And the message isn't lost on the congregation: The really important work here is to serve on a board or committee.

This emphasis on committees not only draws members to manage (instead of minister), it also focuses their attention on themselves (rather than the world around them). When I came to Bear Valley, forty people attended, and the constitution required approximately twenty committees. I was shocked that this struck no one as odd. Everyone groaned about the committees, most of which were not functioning, but it hadn't occurred to them that there might be a better way to run a church. To solve this problem, I insisted — as one of the conditions of my accepting the pastorate — that the church restructure into a single deacon board.

My experience combating committees is not unique. Several years ago I was invited by a pastor friend to attend his church's monthly council meeting. The church had ten boards, and the ten board chairs formed the church council, which led the church. My friend lamented that church members were fighting one another, and the church had almost no ministries beyond its walls. Furthermore, the six to eight internal programs were faltering. Essentially, he said, they didn't know where they were going, and they weren't having any fun getting there.

The council meeting opened with prayer, and then the chairman said, "Let's hear the minutes of the last month's meeting." But before the minutes could be read, one of the council members interrupted: "What is our guest doing here?" The chairman explained that when they finished their business, I would speak about developing strategies for outreach. The questioner responded, "I don't think any outsiders should be in this meeting. What we're discussing here is none of his business."

The chairman, now clearly upset, said, "I really don't care what you think. Let's read the minutes and get on with the meeting."

The antagonist insisted, "No outsiders should be in this meeting, and if you won't ask him to leave, I insist we take a vote."

Two voted for me to leave, four voted for me to stay, and four abstained. The pastor told me later this incident typified the bad blood between the chairman and the other man.

The next week I was speaking in New Mexico, and during a break, two men told me about their ministry in local bars. They pray for an hour two mornings a week and on those evenings spend time in designated bars as "bar chaplains." When we finished talking, the younger man threw his arm over the shoulder of the older man, and they walked off, clearly enjoying their ministry and each other.

As I watched them go, I thought, *What's the difference between these two men and the two I met the previous week?* Then I recalled a speaker's illustration that encouraged people to stay on the front line of ministry. "In war," he explained, "there is only one objective on the front line: defeat the enemy. Everyone pulls together; there's no time to complain. But when you get a few miles behind the front line, everyone is complaining — about the food, the mail, the weather. When you leave the front line, griping becomes a way of life." I realized these two men were front-line officers; the ones I'd met the week before were rear-echelon bureaucrats.

But too often we take our most committed people and make them rear-echelon bureaucrats instead of front-line officers. We produce managers, not ministers. In *Leaders*, Bennis and Nanus observe, "The problem with many organizations, and especially the ones that are failing, is that they tend to be overmanaged and underled." We need to streamline our structures, freeing our leaders to be primarily ministers, not managers.

We begin by encouraging our people to minister, not manage. A key way to do that is to reverse the normal process and highlight those doing ministry. Some churches display pictures of the elder board in the church foyer. We think it's better to put up pictures of people leading ministries. We list the lay leaders of our target ministries on the back of our weekly bulletin and in our visitor's brochure. At our annual Celebration Sunday, a slide show highlights the people involved in our ministries. Occasionally people set up in the foyer displays about their ministries. As a result, although few people can identify our deacons, many recognize the leaders of our ministries.

After a while, that message begins to change things. We have in our congregation a doctor who is a pastor's son. He was raised in the church and believed that playing a significant lay role in the church meant serving on a church board. He has served two terms on our deacon board, in fact. But when he caught the fire for ministry, he decided to open a medical clinic in the inner city. He now earns his living by working half-time in a suburban practice and donates his remaining time at the clinic. I doubt he would accept an invitation to be nominated for the deacon board again, because he's tasted ministry and found it more satisfying than management.

We tell our deacons, "Your management here is critical, because you're the only ones doing it." And we take them on an annual retreat and thank and encourage them there. But we're honest with them: "You're in a context in which managers don't get lots of attention." We have to find deacons who are cut out of true servant material, who can thrive in a behind-the-scenes role. We resonate with Acts 6: Let's find some qualified people who can handle the distribution of funds, so that we can free the others to do the more important work of ministry.

Give Everyone Permission to Minister

Whenever I talk about getting lay people involved in ministry, one of the major concerns is, "How do you train them?" My answer is, "Life has probably already trained them." In our congregation, for example, we have a lawyer who began a mediation ministry. An occupational therapist began serving the physically disabled. Four couples, after reading Ron Sider's *Rich Christians in an Age of Hunger*, began our street ministry. The point is, every one of these people drew upon his or her life experiences to begin an effective ministry.

But in many churches, we pastors are afraid people can't minister until they've been trained, and training, we assume, means giving knowledge as colleges and seminaries give knowledge. (Naturally, we cognitively trained leaders reproduce what we have experienced.) Training means receiving content. As a result, I've found most lay people are convinced they don't have enough knowledge to be real ministers.

But when the focus is on skills, lay people are encouraged: life has given them skills, and they know it. I've watched a host of people who probably wouldn't perform well in the classroom do a great job in ministries. Probably none of the people I mentioned above could define *sacerdotalism*, but they can design, lead, and participate in significant ministries.

So over the years, we've underscored that in the Great Commission Jesus already gave everybody permission to minister. If people want our church to recognize their ministry, however, they must follow four simple guidelines:

1. Don't ask for money (unless you're willing to have your ministry proposal decided by those responsible for the budget).

2. You, not a staff person, must run the ministry. (To put it negatively, you're not at liberty to create monkeys for other people's backs.)

3. Stay out of morally questionable areas.

4. Stay out of doctrinal disputes.

If they adhere to these guidelines, they already have permission to launch the ministry. (The thinking behind these guidelines will be explained further in Chapter 8.)

We seldom have to say no to someone, but if we do, these guidelines keep us from being accused of favoritism. Most of the time, however, the four simple guidelines give people who didn't think *they* could minister the permission to plunge ahead. As a result, nearly all of our outreach ministries have come from the minds and initiatives of lay people. Some members, for example, saw the needs of step-parents and started a support group for them, which has proven tremendously effective in reaching unchurched remarried people.

Don't Train Too Soon

Although effective ministry doesn't require extensive knowledge, training remains helpful. In fact, lay people today have greater training resources available than most clergy have had throughout history. The trick, though, is not marshaling plentiful resources, but timing the training. It's usually best to wait to train people until they are already immersed in ministry. Training doesn't produce ministry. But once God's Spirit moves and ministries begin, training enhances ministry, because people involved in the challenges of daily ministry yearn for greater effectiveness.

When I came to Bear Valley, I introduced the church to Evangelism Explosion. We ran the program and introduced people to Christ. The moment we'd halt the program, however, we wouldn't hear any more stories of members leading others to Christ. The program hadn't developed into a lifestyle.

The problem, I realized, wasn't the program; it's excellent, and we still use it. The problem was the timing. People weren't already involved in the lives of non-Christians, so they didn't fervently want to learn how to share their faith effectively. I wasn't building on what they were already doing. So as long as I called the meetings and got the people out and oiled the machinery, people were won to Christ. But it was incredibly draining since conversions depended on my continually keeping the program cranked up.

Now, we offer training *after* most members are involved in ministry, and I hear about conversions through more natural ways: A young woman who attends our ministry to mothers of preschoolers is led to Christ during lunch. A student from Japan writes to say she's become a Christian through our international-students outreach. The members who take Evangelism Explosion training now usually come hungry to hear because they're involved in a ministry in which they can use the skills.

In addition, we offer MIT (Ministers in Training) — Bible-college courses on topics such as church history and systematic theology. For years we've used the Navigators 2:7 discipleship program, materials from other parachurch groups, and programs we've written ourselves. Recently we've developed a ministry of "spiritual planning," in which we tailor an individual discipleship program to a person's experiences and needs.

However, the primary element needed to do ministry is desire, not training. So we tell people, "You don't need training to do ministry. However, once you're involved in ministry, the training can help you become more effective." And that's when we offer it.

Bend with Building Needs

Separating church ministry from the church building jars many people. And some church-growth adherents unintentionally foster dependence on buildings when they stress the need for parking and large nurseries, and declare the three most important factors of growth are location, location, and location.

We've grown in an inadequate facility in a part of the city where churches haven't grown for over a decade. It's not due to the location or facility; nor have we greater access to God. I attribute our growth to our flexible mind-set. Other things being equal, maybe the three most important things about church growth are flexibility, flexibility, flexibility!

Some of our ministries — particularly music and Christian education — would benefit greatly if we relocated. A contingent on our deacon board occasionally points out the liability of our cramped facilities. We get comments about the lack of adequate parking.

Improved facilities would be nice, but they don't fit our philosophy of ministry. We're not against big buildings, but we don't want to build one simply to house internal ministries such as choirs and Sunday school. We want to look outward, and we've learned we can do that even with fairly limited facilities. We've developed multiple "congregations," and we hold ten services each Sunday morning, one of them at a junior high school.

A Long Journey Begins with Patience

Options for ministry abound. Every hurting and confused part of the culture represents a great opportunity. The average church can become a powerhouse of ministries penetrating the culture. But the process won't happen overnight.

I began teaching these principles in 1971, and it was 1977 before we started our first ministries beyond our walls. It took six years to create the necessary mind-set to mobilize people for ministry. But God is not in a rush. The most important thing is to get started in the right direction.

A man in our church wanted to set up country-club dinner parties to reach unchurched executives. He had connections with some of Denver's prominent business people, and we were excited about the prospect for outreach. We announced a brainstorming meeting for anyone interested in the ministry. Nobody came.

A year and a half later we announced another start-up meeting for such a ministry, and a few people came. At the first dinner, eighty executives turned in cards indicating a decision for Christ, a desire to join a Bible study, or a request for more information.

For some reason, we got put on hold for eighteen months. But when the ministry began, it took off. We were reminded to stay close to the Head and wait for him to release the desire to minister.

In churches positioned to evangelize, members have confidence in the church and feel comfortable inviting outsiders to the services. Growing churches have built a culture that views evangelism as the norm.

— Calvin C. Ratz

CHAPTER FIVE

Preparing People as Witnesses

Walking down the first fairway at a golf club, Don, a recent convert, told me about his work. He ran his own business, specializing in securing high-profile managers and executives for large corporations. "When they need a certain type of person," he said, "they come to me. People call me a headhunter."

That caught my attention. As I plotted how to land my four irons on the greens, I also thought about my job. Yes, I'm called to preach, pray, and visit the sick. But finding people to fill jobs—and finding jobs in which to place people—is a critical part of my ministry. I, too, am a headhunter.

More specifically, one ministry to which I am called to recruit people is evangelism. One church leader put the challenge this way: "I have no difficulty getting my people to serve on a church committee, sing in the choir, or even teach a Sunday school class, but how can I get them involved in sharing their faith with others? How do I prepare my people to witness?"

Whose Job to Witness?

Preparing people to witness begins with a conviction that lay people make the best witnesses, mostly because they are more strategically located to witness than ministers. So, if extensive evangelism is going to happen, it's going to happen through them.

Tom is a mechanic who came to the Lord a couple of years ago. Many of his friends continue to drop by to talk about old times. One of his friends, a truck driver named Gord, was an introvert. He had no personal church experience, but he did have strong opinions about preachers and what he *thought* went on in church. The idea of conversing with a preacher turned him off.

However, Gord was intrigued by the change in Tom and started asking questions. Tom told Gord what had happened to him and how he could experience the same thing. Gord and his wife eventually came to the church with Tom's family, and then Tom brought them to see me. We talked for a couple of hours, setting them at ease and sharing the way of salvation. The next week we met again, and Gord and his wife each committed themselves to Christ. The final decision was made in my office, but it was Tom who had brought them to a place of faith.

Tom's friends were not afraid or intimidated by him. He was unencumbered by the negative images outsiders have of preachers and the church. In addition, he had just experienced a radical change in his life that was noticed by non-Christians. It's the Toms in our churches who are the keys to evangelism, and growing churches are committed to helping their Toms reach their friends for Christ.

Consequently, evangelism in our church is primarily a lay

ministry, a function of the whole church, a cooperative effort between pastor and people. If we limit our outreach to the specialists,
the platform personalities, or the itinerant evangelists, we end up
bottlenecking our growth. So, we try to create an environment in
which lay evangelism is expected, and a large percentage of our
people are involved in personal evangelism.

But this conviction about the priority of lay evangelism is not
enough. We also have a strategy to make it an ongoing reality.

Make Evangelism Part of the Church Culture

One personnel executive told me, "Every company has its
own culture. Some corporate cultures foster growth; others inhibit
it. A positive corporate culture is the glue that holds the team together and engenders an atmosphere where creativity and achievement are the norm."

Church culture is no less important. Every church has its
unique identity and group values. It shows up in the way people
think and talk about themselves as a church. Churches that feel
good about themselves are positioned to evangelize, because members have confidence in the church and feel comfortable inviting
outsiders to the services. Growing churches have built a culture that
views evangelism as the norm, not a marginalized anomaly.

Excitement about evangelism can be created in a variety of
ways, but one of my friends who pastors a vibrant church puts it
best: "Excitement for evangelism starts with the pastor and leadership team of the church. Only then will it infect the congregation."

As pastor I try to bring the evangelistic vision into sharp focus.
I say and model the message: "There's an exciting job to be done,
and with God's help, we can do it." I talk, practice, and encourage
evangelism.

Working with the church leaders, I've tried to build excitement about evangelism into the culture of our church in a variety of
ways:

● *We've made evangelism our theme for an entire year.* We talked
about evangelism and built a heavy evangelistic component into
everything we did, including special outreach activities in every

department. In Sunday services, we featured guests who were known for both their appeal to outsiders and their ability to gather a harvest.

That year we distributed gummed labels with the phrases, EVERYONE A MINISTER and I'M A LAY MINISTER IN TRAINING. I still see the labels on refrigerators and the covers of Bibles. The labels keep evangelism in the minds of the people.

● *We've encouraged ordinary Christians to share their faith.* Most Christians feel inadequate to witness and need reassurance about their ability to lead someone to Jesus Christ.

People need my encouragement, but they are more excited by living examples of evangelism taking place through the lives of others in the church. Consequently, we find people with positive witnessing experiences to share their stories during our Sunday services. Such testimonies are often the high point of a service.

● *We've stretched the old guard.* Perhaps the hardest people to excite about evangelism are Christians who've been around the church for twenty years. They've heard it all. Sometimes they're cynical, and often they're the most fearful about witnessing.

Exciting these veterans without antagonizing them is a delicate process. The key is getting them to do something that stretches their faith but is not so threatening it scares them away.

We saw a tremendous change in some of these evangelism drones as they participated in a prayer-visitation program. It wasn't raw evangelism, but it did involve calling on church families they didn't know. As we recruited the callers, most of whom never had done anything like this before, it was obvious they were terrified.

The visits were parceled over a three-week period, but by the end of the first week, many callers returned asking for more homes to visit. They were excited by what they had accomplished. Those prayer visits helped build confidence, so that now, many are prepared to take on other ministries that involve contacting strangers. Successfully completed ministry at this level built confidence to take on personal witnessing.

● *We also publicly announce our priorities.* At the conclusion of worship, I often encourage my people to make a difference in the world through the power of Jesus Christ. It's a continual reminder that ministry takes place outside the church as well as in it. I want our people to leave our services feeling, *With God's help, we can witness.*

● *We use positive motivation.* A church culture that breathes excitement about evangelism can't be built on guilt. Enthusiasm is created by seeing possibilities, by seeing what God is already doing and by recognizing the thrill that leading a person to Christ brings. I find it easy to slip into guilt-producing vocabulary when trying to encourage my people to share their faith. But lately I've been working to eliminate vocabulary that produces unnecessary guilt: "If you don't evangelize . . ." or "You should . . ." In addition, through preaching, bulletin articles, and personal contacts, I underscore that ordinary Christians without a theological degree not only can lead a friend to faith, but also that sharing our faith is the most fulfilling thing we can do.

It's so thrilling when people catch the vision for evangelism. Recently we've been talking about retooling some longstanding programs to have a stronger evangelistic component. I knew we were getting through when one of our experienced members asked me, "When are we starting with this new emphasis? I want to be a part of what's happening."

Make Enlistment a Top Priority

Great sports teams are built through solid recruiting. Teams that consistently win replenish their ranks each year with quality young players.

The same is true in the church. Great churches don't grow by chance; evangelism happens when people are recruited and then channeled into ministries that make it possible for them to make contact with those outside the church.

It's not easy to enlist people into evangelism ministry. Witnessing can be the most intimidating thing a believer can do. Often it's necessary to overcome apathy, fear, and even some theological misunderstandings to get people involved.

Preaching and other platform ministries can create interest, but it's personal recruiting that activates a church's evangelism ministry. Here are some things I've learned about enlisting others in evangelism.

1. Enlist through prayer. Jesus said, "Ask the Lord of the harvest therefore to send out workers into his harvest field." Some have made those words the domain of world missions, but they apply to local evangelism just as much as the call to foreign missions.

One of my staff had been frustrated for several months trying to locate a new leader for one of our children's programs. Under the previous leader, the program had become ingrown, self-serving, and a barrier to new folk coming into the church. We saw this as a time to refocus this ministry to include a stronger evangelistic component.

One morning, as he was praying about this position, he thought of a person neither of us previously had considered. It was obvious this person could do the job, and the next day he was approached. He accepted, and he turned the program around. A ministry that had become self-contained now has an outward focus, and the right recruit came through prayer.

2. Enlist new converts. Established church members may be good people, strong financial supporters of the church's ministries, and even involved in running some of the existing programs of the church. But many are just not into talking about their faith to non-Christians.

New converts do. They take to sharing their faith naturally, so we don't want to make the mistake of putting them to work staffing programs that serve the existing church.

Gary became a Christian a couple of years ago. Having few church connections, he immediately began sharing his faith outside the church. Within a year he brought a dozen of his family and friends to Christ.

One of our staff members recognized what was happening, so he encouraged Gary. He spent time helping him learn how to share his faith more and more effectively. Consequently, Gary continued to influence others. If we'd guided this new convert to meet the needs of existing Christians, we'd have lost a prime opportunity.

3. Enlist personally. Jesus' disciples weren't volunteers. They were painstakingly chosen one by one. It takes time, but there's no short cut in effective recruiting. Announcements from the pulpit or blurbs in the bulletin rarely produce good recruits. Most good evangelism workers are individually recruited.

Individual recruiting is especially important in encouraging shy and reticent people to share their faith. Many timid people never will volunteer. But when we approach them personally, their confidence increases. Often, these folk are gifted and qualified. They simply need to be drawn into the work through personal contact and reassurance.

I've stopped recruiting in the rush after a service. It leaves the recruit with the impression that he was just the first one I came across. The best recruiting takes place away from the church building, when attention is more focused. People tend to respond to a task and perform in ministry according to the way they are recruited. Elevating the process of recruiting not only shows the potential recruit the seriousness of the task, but it also secures a higher level of commitment when the assignment is accepted.

4. Enlist to specific tasks with a time limit. When recruiting individuals for evangelistic ministry, particularly leadership positions, we've discovered the recruit needs to know exactly what he's being asked to do. So we've developed written job descriptions for all the leadership positions in the church. That eliminates later confusion.

Putting a time limit on leadership positions also helps recruitment. Some hesitate to take on a new assignment because they're afraid that once started, they won't know how to get out of the job gracefully. Too many have taken on a Sunday school class only to find themselves stuck with it twelve years later.

Consequently, all our leadership positions are annual appointments. This gives us an out every year if we need to make a change. It also means a recruit can leave a position gracefully without appearing a quitter.

5. Enlist to lifestyle evangelism. Some free spirits never will fit the mold of organized programs, though such people may possess a strong bent for evangelism. In fact, most evangelism takes place in the normal flow of life, outside the framework of the congregation's programs.

For example, one member of the church family, Bill recently had a business lunch with an acquaintance. The conversation eventually turned to spiritual matters. Over a sandwich and several cups of coffee, he had convinced his friend to trust in Christ.

When ordinary believers, in the normal course of life, respond to the prompting of the Holy Spirit to share their faith, great things happen. Preparing a congregation for evangelism means challenging and preparing each believer to seize such opportunities.

Enlisting people for evangelism is an ongoing job. Although we recruit annually for all our ministries, recruitment isn't left at that. It's at the top of my own job description, and it's the mind-set I try to instill in my staff.

Train for Evangelism Continually

In his book, *Thriving on Chaos*, Tom Peters says, "Training has been IBM's secret weapon for decades. At one point, the senior Watson had just a one-person staff — an education director. An ad last year featured an IBM worker at the company's Lexington, Kentucky, site who had undergone major retraining a half-dozen times in a twenty-five year career to fend off technical obsolescence."

Whether it's IBM or Disney World, growing companies spend lavishly on training. They've learned that taking a person off the job and sending him through a training program not only increases his productivity, it also builds confidence and morale. Training costs are an integral part of annual budgets in successful companies.

In much the same way, training in the church has to be planned and budgeted. Sadly, many congregations spend a great deal on buildings and maintenance but little time and only a minimal amount of their annual budgets on developing people for ministry, especially evangelistic ministry. Yet we can't afford not to train our people. Setting aside time and money for training may mean short-term inconvenience and cost, but long-range payoffs ensue.

We now include several thousand dollars in our annual budget for conferences and seminars that provide training for staff and members. We're prepared to assist financially people who attend training seminars outside our church. In our annual church calendar, we also set aside time for training workshops.

Training has to be continual. There's no such thing as a one-time training program that fits all the people for a lifetime of ministry. Aggressive corporations don't simply retrain staff to avoid obsolescence but to maintain sharpness and commitment in their employees. Because we forget much of what we learn, ongoing training is essential to keep important information up front.

In order to build evangelism into every church department, we include evangelism training in the regular training we give to each department. Sunday school teachers are shown how to lead children to Jesus Christ, not just tell Bible stories. Our Wee College, a program for preschool children, is designed to lead children to faith in Jesus Christ, not just creatively teach them.

During Sunday school classes, we're teaching our adults and youth how to witness, and we even practice witnessing to each other. The fear of failure, the fear of rejection, and the fear of people are accentuated in the church. People don't want to disappoint a pastor or fail God in some way. Well-defined training programs go a long way in overcoming fear and building confidence.

Our training has three dimensions. First, *we prepare people spiritually.* Character creates credibility, and intimacy with God builds intensity, all of which makes for effective evangelism.

Training for evangelism, then, starts with spiritual disciplines and spiritual vitality. We begin by teaching people how to read the Bible and pray — genuinely.

This doesn't mean people must attain a superior level of spirituality before they begin to minister. If that were the case, few of us would qualify. But a solid spiritual base must be established from which they can mature. After that, involvement in ministry spurs further spiritual growth. Knowing that others are watching is a great incentive for maturity and growth.

Second, *we prepare people factually.* Historically, a lack of information hasn't been our problem. Many churches have been filled with overstuffed Christians who do little with their biblical knowledge.

But times are changing. There has been a significant decrease in Bible literacy, even among the churched. Our experience-oriented society places little emphasis on information. Our children and young adults may have genuine experiences with God but often little logical understanding of the Scriptures to back up that experience.

So, many new converts bring nearly complete ignorance of the Bible and spiritual principles. One 45-year-old man who has been a Christian for two years and has attended church regularly jolted me with the question, "Pastor, I'm confused. Did Moses live before or after Jesus?"

Evangelism training programs, then, can't make many assumptions about a Christian's knowledge. If we're going to train people to share their faith, we have to make sure they understand their faith, as well as the techniques of sharing it.

Third, *we prepare people practically.* People need specific ways to share their faith. For example, if asked by a friend to explain how to become a Christian, many believers could give an adequate answer. However, those same people have trouble turning a secular conversation to spiritual things. They know how to answer the question, "What must I do to be saved?" but they don't know how to get a friend to ask the question.

We teach our people to move conversations gently to spiritual concerns and then to ask questions like: "How would you describe a real Christian?" and "Do you ever think about God or religious things?" The answers to these nonthreatening questions clearly indicate a person's understanding of the Christian faith. The more tools such as these that people have at their disposal, the more they'll activate their witness.

I encourage people to ask this question when appropriate: "Would you like me to tell you the difference Jesus Christ has made in my life?" It certainly arouses curiosity. In some of our training classes, we have people write out and memorize a sixty-second testimony on "what Jesus Christ means to me."

Another question: "Would you like to know how Jesus Christ can make a difference in your life?" Again, we believe it's important for people to be ready to give a simple explanation of the gospel. We encourage the use of Billy Graham's "Steps to Peace with God." It's understandable and covers all the basics, and Billy Graham's imprint immediately engenders trust among many to whom we witness.

In addition, we've run a six-week course for those who counsel the people who respond to our altar calls. The training emphasized the critical nature of such counseling, the spiritual preparation required, the logistics of counseling in our church, and the special methods of counseling people who respond to a public appeal.

Successful training requires a training mind-set among the pastoral staff. Training is at the top of the job description of every one of our staff members. It's not so much the programs we run as the atmosphere in which we counsel and interact with people that encourages people to start sharing their faith.

Consequently, some training takes place through the staff's informal contacts with the members. For example, the other night my wife and I were having coffee with a church couple. Unplanned, the conversation turned to a discussion of their ministries. As we talked, I was called on to answer some questions this couple had about their church work. Though it was informal, this talk probably accomplished as much as a structured training session. Because it was personalized, I was able to apply my answers to that couple. Our staff is constantly on the lookout for such opportunities.

Encourage People to Persevere

Keeping people involved in evangelistic ministry is as critical as recruiting them to ministry. I'm thankful that it's also easier. Retailers say that it takes five times more effort and expense to get a new customer than it does to maintain an existing customer. Likewise, I'm learning it takes less effort to motivate and encourage existing workers in the church than to recruit and train new ones.

These volunteers don't work for pay, but neither do they work for free. Church workers, particularly those whose ministry is evangelism, are a special breed, a valued resource. They need to be handled with care.

Releasing people into ministry doesn't mean abandoning them. When Jesus sent the disciples out two by two, he set them free to preach, witness, and heal. But when they came back, he took them aside to refresh them. I imagine he offered encouragement and assessment, as well as further teaching and instruction. He likely celebrated their victories and answered their questions.

I encourage my people by trying to be present and involved in their ministries. I show up often enough to indicate I care and absent myself enough to show I trust them.

Most new programs, particularly those associated with evangelism, stall around the nine- to fifteen-month mark when the reality of launching a new program settles in. Sometimes there's opposition or misunderstanding. Sometimes there's conflict with other programs. Some good people just don't have what it takes to sustain a new program.

One cure for discouragement is pastoral encouragement to combat the inertia that plagues almost every new program. Normally it doesn't take a lot to encourage workers. Most compliments take less than a minute. I make every effort to thank people and celebrate what they're doing to help the church to grow. Public recognition is invaluable.

More than Technique

I believe more people are lost to ministry because they are challenged too little than because they're asked to do too much. My desire is to give people freedom to minister, not just to fill a position. I want to give them substantive ministry, not a token.

When I do that, and back them with encouragement that's genuine and expectations that are high, they will witness to the hope that is within them.

Randy, a sharp, young executive, was climbing the corporate ladder. It seemed he was getting a promotion every few months. But Randy's heart was in serving God and sharing his faith. He wasn't afraid to talk to his colleagues about his Lord.

Randy and I spent hours together discussing church work, the meaning of Bible verses, and ways to serve God. Whether it was in my office or after a strenuous game of racquetball, we tossed around ways of sharing our faith and making contact with those outside the church.

One Saturday evening a pastor from a neighboring church phoned to say he was seriously ill and asked if I had someone to preach for him the next morning. I gave Randy a call, and though he'd never preached before, he agreed to do his best. He stayed up most of the night studying and praying, and then spoke the following morning. He did a respectable job, I heard. And the unleashing of his talents brought growth and expanded his appetite for ministry.

In the end, of course, it's the Holy Spirit who excites God's people and mobilizes them into an army of spiritually motivated lay evangelists. He creates an internal motivation, a lasting excitement, and a sense of urgency.

We can't take the place of the Holy Spirit. He's sovereign and moves in ways we'll never fully understand. But we must always acknowledge and make room for the Spirit's ministry, for he is the ultimate motivator for evangelism. Without him, our efforts at rousing an apathetic church are futile.

Our task is to discover the untapped resources already within the congregation. I wanted a way to draw out from each person what God had especially equipped that individual to do.

— Frank Tillapaugh

CHAPTER SIX

Getting the Right People in the Right Places

I want to get involved, but I don't know where I fit."

"I'm not ready to do ministry. In fact, I could use some ministry to *me* first."

"I want to do something, but I'm not sure I have anything to offer."

We all hear such comments often in ministry. I recognize them as expressions of a basic Christian need: to be useful and adequately equipped for ministry.

The church's traditional approach — fitting people into existing slots in the church's ministry — doesn't always meet this need. Nor have I found spiritual gifts classes, growth institutes, or seminars particularly helpful in encouraging and equipping lay people to reach out. Instead, they've often received a mish-mash of material, a muddle of messages, but no clear direction on what to do next.

Consequently, I began to look for a model that represented how the church could better meet this need, helping people become involved in useful ministries. I worked from two assumptions: (1) God has entrusted to each believer the necessary resources for what he has called that person to do. (2) God has given each church the people necessary to do what he has called that church to do. Our task is to discover the untapped resources already within the congregation. I wanted a way to draw out from each person what God had especially equipped that individual to do.

I looked for models of a structured but personalized approach. In the end, a financial planning model seemed appropriate. When people plan their finances, they first analyze their assets and liabilities. Then they develop a plan that will make the most of their financial resources. Through the efforts of two of our pastors at Bear Valley, Tim Robertson and Ron Oertli, this idea was developed and applied to personal resources. We called it "Spiritual Planning."

There are three phases of the planning process. First, we ask each person to take inventory of the resources God has entrusted to him or her (like spiritual gifts, natural talents, and acquired skills). Then we propose potential ministries (based on the church's needs and available opportunities) and job descriptions. Finally, we help the individual write a specific plan of action for the next twelve months. This plan includes measurable, attainable goals for growth and ministry as well as a system of accountability.

No doubt, other churches would do it differently, but here are the steps we use.

Taking Inventory

Linda had been a Christian for several years, but not serious about her faith. One day, she explained why to me. "I'm not sure I have anything to offer the church. I have no idea what special gifts or talents I might have. In fact, I'm not sure God even gave me any."

Rather than immediately find Linda a position or program to work in, we decided the better way would be to help her discover the spiritual resources God had placed in her keeping. For example, Linda had been divorced recently and was feeling useless to Christ as a result. Instead, we pointed out that this life experience could be the beginning of her resource inventory.

An inventory of resources is more than a list of experiences, however. One man effectively taught trigonometry at a public high school. But he was frustrated when, in light of his experience, his church asked him to teach a Bible class; he was not an effective Bible teacher. Spiritual gifts and acquired skills are two different things, but both must be included in a person's resource inventory.

In addition to natural talents, specialized training, and life experience, people also have God-cultivated concerns about others' needs which intrigue them or keep them awake at night or drive them to action. Burdens for others give them goals and aspirations. These things together — experiences, gifts, aspirations — we call the "resource mix."

At Bear Valley, people attend four sessions with one of our trained spiritual planners. The first three sessions focus on the resource mix. Before the first session, we give each person a questionnaire. It must be completed prior to the first session and covers a number of key areas.

The questionnaire also screens out the merely semi-interested because it requires extensive thought to complete. After looking it over, some people cancel their first appointment because they're not ready to give serious thought to finding their place. We've found those people probably would not act on their discoveries even if they complete the process. On the other hand, those ready to serve find the questionnaire stimulating.

The Survey

The ten questions on the inventory explore spiritual growth from many angles. We encourage people to write their answers, but if that's too daunting, we let them think through the questions and come prepared to discuss them.

1. Describe your personal, spiritual pilgrimage. What led to your conversion to Christ? What formal and informal training has contributed to your growth? What crises have you weathered? What have been your experiences in ministry? Also mention individuals who have greatly influenced you.

2. Is God "cultivating a concern" in you for ministry? What specific needs, issues, or situations particularly touch your heart? Do these concerns make you want to "roll up your sleeves" and go to work?

3. Up to now, what concrete steps have you taken to address these needs or get involved in these issues?

4. What do you believe is the general purpose of this process?

5. Specifically identify several things you expect to accomplish through this process.

6. Set aside these expectations for the moment and *dream*. Assume you had all the resources you wanted and needed, and that God would guarantee your success in anything you wanted to do. Describe what your life would look like ten years from now. Who would you be? What would you be doing?

7. Identify several resources God has entrusted to you (e.g., spiritual gifts, natural talents, acquired skills, experiences).

8. What is your greatest strength?

9. Are there any present barriers keeping you from living up to your God-given potential? If so, identify them.

10. Where do you need to grow the most?

The Sessions

During the first spiritual planning session, we go over the answers to the questionnaire. We ask permission to take notes on what individuals say and then move through the questions. We ask people to clarify or expand answers we don't fully understand.

Then, typically, the leader will ask people if the process, so far, is meeting their needs. He'll also give them permission to drop out at this stage if they've discerned this is not what they need. He encourages them to continue, and promises to work with those who do so. He reminds them, as well, of the exciting discoveries that lay ahead.

By giving people permission to back out, we give those who are not ready a graceful way out; we also increase the commitment of those who stay. By the fourth session, those who remain will then be open and ready for spiritual direction.

At the end of session one, we briefly go over the Meyers/Briggs Type Indicator question book and answer sheet. We give an envelope with postage on it. People complete the MBTI and mail it back to us before the second session.

In session two we analyze the results of the type indicator and explain the implications. The Meyers/Briggs Type Indicator analyzes people according to four continuums, each of which describes a personality trait: Extroversion-Introversion; Sensing-INtuition; Thinking-Feeling; Judging-Perceiving. There are many combinations, each of which are summarized in four letters, one for each dominate trait the person displays. (For example, one person on one end of each continuum would be described as an ESTJ, at the other end, INFP, and somewhere in the middle, ESFP.) Naturally, we don't pigeon hole people or make definitive statements, but use language like "You *tend* to make decisions this way." Often, people find this analysis the most helpful thing we do in all four sessions. It gives them a clear and concise way to perceive and understand their God-given personalities.

At the end of session two, we provide information on spiritual gifts — listing those in the Bible. Then we ask each person to talk to others during the week about the impression he or she gives. How do others perceive him? What gifts do they feel she has? This provides interesting, sometimes surprising, information for people.

During the third session, we discuss spiritual gifts. We teach what the Bible says regarding spiritual gifts and encourage individuals to experiment and, within the context of ministry, discover their gifts for ministry. We discuss areas in which people have excelled in the past. We try to help people discover not one single gift, but a gift mix of two or three.

In addition, we try to notice patterns among all elements: life experience, acquired skills, and spiritual gifts. Brian Hathaway, pastor of The Atatu Bible Chapel in New Zealand, once observed that King David used his natural talent (music) to soothe a troubled king, his acquired skill (sling) to slay a ferocious enemy, and his spiritual gift (leadership) to produce a triumphant period in Israel's history. Likewise, we believe God provides each person a unique resource mix.

At the end of our third session, we give a printed description of all the ministries of Bear Valley Baptist Church and the specific jobs within each ministry. In addition, we encourage people to imagine ministries they'd like to be involved in that don't exist — yet.

The participants leave session three with two assignments. First, based on what they've learned, they pick three or four ministries that interest them. Second, they write an action plan.

A Plan of Action

An action plan is a specific, written procedure for spiritual growth and ministry. This "spiritual plan" lists goals for the next twelve months in seven areas: worship, instruction, fellowship, ministry, stewardship, family/friends, and personal development. We discuss the action plans at session four.

Since every person is unique, each final product takes on a different form. One artistically inclined woman presented her written plan in the form of a creative collage, while an engineer, Pat, came in with a four-page computerized printout. Others scribble their action plans on napkins.

Whatever the means, we want people to list attainable and measurable goals. For instance, here are the types of goals people set in each area.

● *Worship.* This includes both corporate and personal worship. One person may promise to attend Sunday worship more regularly, even when traveling on business or vacation. Another may decide to have personal devotions ten to fifteen minutes a day, five days a week. Again, we're not looking for extravagant goals, but ones that are simple, manageable, measurable.

• *Instruction.* This category embraces participation in a Sunday school class or small-group Bible study, or following a "reading plan." One person may commit to reading two books a month. Another may decide to listen to tapes that feature a Christian speaker. One fellow chose to go to a seminar on leading small groups, a gift he wanted to nurture.

• *Fellowship.* A Sunday school class or Bible study group may include fellowship as well as instruction. A church softball league may also suffice. The point is we need one another and sometimes must deliberately plan fellowship to make it happen.

• *Ministry.* After people have chosen three or four options from our opportunity list, they choose one ministry they will likely participate in. This goal describes when, who, and how ministry will be engaged in. We encourage people to try a particular ministry at least three months to see if the fit is right.

In addition to the niche in the church they are going to experiment with, we challenge people to begin praying for one personal relationship they can cultivate, with God's help, as a ministry. They may not even know the person at this time, but we want them to pray about the opportunity. Over the next twelve months, they are encouraged to nurture that relationship for the sole purpose of sharing the gospel. We do it not so they can add a scalp to their belts, but rather to experience the adventure of personal evangelism, which is part of ministry, as well.

• *Stewardship.* This encompasses use of time and money. A minimum goal is to tithe. If people are tithing, they may choose to increase their percentage.

At this point, we often discover that someone is deep in debt, which has strapped their giving. In this case, a person may decide to meet with a financial counselor and become a better manager of financial resources.

We also ask people to be good stewards of their time. So another goal may involve cutting down the amount of overtime one works to give more time to ministry. Others feel called to cut back church involvement for the sake of family. Chuck was miraculously saved out of a drug culture. He was so excited about his faith that he jumped from one ministry to another, one fellowship group to another, and he never stayed with one thing long enough to truly benefit. In addition, he wasn't spending enough time at home. During spiritual planning Chuck asked, "I need some fine tuning. What do you think?" Because of the spiritual planning process, one of our pastors (Chuck's spiritual planner) was free to say, "You need to withdraw from your small-group Bible study. You're getting plenty of instruction in the seminary classes you're taking. At this point, regular time with your wife is more important than the extra instruction."

Balancing family, career, church, and community is difficult. At times we simply encourage a commitment to ongoing evaluation — committing, for instance, to sit down each month to discuss the balance with family members. Most people find this feasible (and measureable).

● *Family and close friends.* We ask each person to list particular goals in regard to their family and friends. Some couples decide to have a date one night each week. One man vowed to travel to see both of his adult sons within the next year. He had not been a Christian when they were growing up, and so it was important to him that they see his lifestyle now.

One single woman who yearned to be married decided, with the encouragement of her spiritual planner, to change her hair style and work on her weight problem; she wanted to look as attractive as God made her to be.

● *Personal development.* We also ask people to accomplish something they have always dreamed about but have never done. One person finally took banjo lessons. Another man climbed a number of Colorado's 14,000-foot mountain peaks. Any kind of development that stretches someone personally is encouraged.

Workable Accountability

This plan works, of course, only if accountability is built into the process. We've tried to prevent the staff or the spiritual planner being the ones holding people accountable. Otherwise, when people are accountable to us, we notice that they disappear around corners when we wave to them at church!

Instead, we've tried to build an accountability system with peers of the same gender. A couple might choose another couple, but in most cases, the wife and husband each choose somebody different. In any case, each person is asked to identify a peer or mentor who will serve as an "accountability partner." A minimum of four meetings (one per quarter) are scheduled during the year, about which the church office gently reminds people by postcard.

The accountability people act as mirrors, not judges. They hold up the plan and help people look objectively at their goals and analyze their success at fulfilling them. If people aren't meeting their goals, the accountability people simply ask, "Why?" They don't dole out punishment; they discuss reasons. They suggest possibilities: "Do you think you should call your spiritual planner back and redefine the goal?" "Do you think this goal is stretching you enough?"

Does It Work?

An effective plan is one that does two things: (1) results in a more dedicated and distinctively Christian lifestyle in people, and (2) puts people in specialized ministries. Sharon is one example of how the system has worked.

Sharon had a background in Christian education. She had taken seminary courses and taught Sunday school classes. But this ministry did not fulfill her. During her spiritual planning process, we learned several key facts about Sharon: she had expertise in computers and could write programs in four languages. In addition, she was concerned about, among other things, people withdrawing from cults.

Bear Valley has a ministry called Shield of Faith which targets people coming out of cults and aberrant Christian groups. And, at the time, Shield of Faith desperately needed someone to work with their computers — a matched set! Later, when Sharon's career led her to another city, she wrote us that the spiritual planning process was some of her most beneficial time spent in Denver.

Many people, of course, are involved in Sunday school classes and other normal church activities when they begin the planning process. And many, as a result, don't change their commitments. But afterward, they're engaged with greater purpose. Many now say, "I know why I'm doing what I'm doing."

And that not only strengthens them, it also solidifies the whole church.

Discouragement is not, in itself, a problem. Anyone who engages in challenging work will become discouraged from time to time. Discouragement becomes a problem, however, when it blurs vision for ministry.

— Myron Augsburger

CHAPTER SEVEN
Maintaining Momentum

D. L. Moody, the great evangelist, was said to have prayed often that the Lord would "keep him from ever losing the wonder."

Anyone who ministers for Christ knows that wonder, as did Moody. We are filled with it when people we serve respond with joy to Christ's love. But the same ministry that fills us with wonder sometimes makes us wonder. Enlivening the souls of others often tries our own. We can become disheartened, and ministry gets mired.

There are a number of things that can stall outreach ministry — fatigue, boredom, a change of priorities, church squabbles, to name a few. But perhaps the most significant is discouragement that accompanies the loss of purpose.

Throughout my ministry, I've tried to sustain not only my own momentum, but also that of people I've walked with, led, or pastored. Here are a few things I have learned.

What Brakes Momentum

Since Christians are in the business of spirituality, so to speak, we are apt to blame a slowdown of momentum on lack of devotion, some moral lapse, or, perhaps, the Devil. Such things can and often do discourage us from reaching out. Naturally, in such cases, prayer and spiritual renewal go a long way toward building momentum again.

On the other hand, we've learned that physical factors also play a role. If I've been up until midnight three nights in a row and then have to get up for a six o'clock appointment, it affects my mood. I become more clipped with others, work seems an effort, and the slightest problem can demoralize me. To put it another way, ministry bogs down when I don't lie down enough.

Aside from spiritual and physical factors, however, I've found people are unusually discouraged from reaching out by one of four factors:

● *Unrealistic goals.* In their yearning to be faithful to Christ, churches often set goals they cannot possibly meet. We think we are being faithful to the upward call, when all we are doing is making the call impossible. If we vow to eradicate poverty in our area of the city, discouragement is inevitable. Better to say, "We will help families in poverty with the means we have available." That is hard enough, but it is something we can do.

Goals also become unrealistic when we insist on perfection: we will help *every* family in our area, at *every* opportunity, using adequately *all* our resources. We cannot do that. We're going to overlook some needs. We're going to waste some of our resources. We will have to turn away some needy people. We might as well admit it up front and save ourselves some discouragement.

Also, some goals prove inaccurate measures of the success of ministry. To aim to give a bag of groceries to every family that asks will dishearten us if we see the same people coming to us month after month for more food. We may have succeeded at giving out groceries, but we will not have succeeded at helping people feed themselves without our aid.

In short, unrealistic goals will discourage us, and that will stall our outreach.

● *Unmeasurable ministries.* Only a few things can be measured in Christian ministry — attendance at meetings, dollars raised, dollars spent. Often the most important things cannot be measured.

Washington, D.C., has one of the highest murder rates in the United States. Naturally, we would like to lower the number of murders in our area of the city, but how do we measure success? Even if the murder rate goes up, we may, nonetheless, have been instrumental in stopping another dozen murders, which would have made the rate even higher.

The same is true of other goals we might set. How do we know how many people we've kept from suicide? How many teenage pregnancies have we prevented? How many people have not started drugs because of our ministry? The list goes on. There are many aspects of ministry that cannot be measured, for which number goals cannot be set. But sometimes when people cannot measure the effect of their work, they get discouraged.

Ministry, of course, is sometimes noticeably successful. Attendance at services is one of the easily measured achievements. But frequently the success is subtle, like salt that seasons food: You can't see it. You cannot measure with the naked eye. But it makes a difference.

Most of the friends of one teenage girl in our church either are or have been pregnant. But not her. She says her lifestyle is different; she is not going to live that way. Where did she get those convictions? Not from her neighborhood, which inadvertently conspires to undermine them. Her convictions have been molded and reinforced by her mother and the Christian community. That is success, but it can't be put on a graph.

● *Inflexible temperaments.* Some people claim that overwork brings discouragement in ministry. That is true to some degree, and we try to deal with that problem when it arises. But it is also true that hard work, in itself, never discouraged anybody; it's the sense of worry, futility, isolation, or lack of appreciation accompanying hard work that will bring discouragement. The deeper issue, then, is not that people are busy, but how they handle their busyness.

I've found some of the most discouraged people tend to be inflexible. The people who get the most accomplished, and find the greatest satisfaction in it, tend to be flexible people.

Why are we told that if we want to get something done, we should ask a busy person to do it? Because they are flexible; they know how to adjust their schedules to meet new demands.

The unbusy person, on the other hand, often is inflexible. Such people live by routine: they rise, take a shower, eat breakfast, read the paper, go to work, have lunch, come home, eat dinner, watch TV, and go to bed, all at appointed hours. If their routine is interrupted, they become flustered. If given an extra task, they can't figure out how to change their schedules to accommodate it.

This, of course, is a caricature. But if we can model flexibility and encourage that trait in others, we will help defeat discouragement.

● *Inappropriate jobs.* If you put a multitalented person in a job for which he has no talents, you're looking for discouragement. Conversely, if you put a single-talented person in the one job that will use his talents, you'll see motivation for years to come.

One young man connected with the college where I was president taught chemistry, but he was not succeeding. He was a good chemist, but he didn't do the one thing teachers need to do: get his students excited about learning. Naturally, his teaching meandered along.

However, he was a gifted researcher, and his ability to analyze and sift through information to find the most relevant data was outstanding. So, the dean and I negotiated with him and moved him from teacher to director of institutional research. He not only worked with enthusiasm, but his work became recognized widely among small liberal arts colleges.

Spotting Burnout Is a Community Concern

Actually, discouragement is not, in itself, a problem. Anyone who engages in challenging work will become discouraged from time to time. Discouragement becomes a problem, however, when it blurs vision for ministry. That's when it can lead to burnout. When people are so discouraged they're ready to quit, outreach ministry will limp along.

Signs of burnout are many: Physically, people often experience more headaches and are lethargic about work. Mentally, they lack creativity, become easily impatient with co-workers, forget to do jobs or meet appointments, and find it difficult to follow through on projects.

However, although it's easy to list signs of burnout on the printed page, it's often difficult — in the scurrying about of weekly activities — to notice the signs in others. That's why in our church, spotting burnout is a community affair. We use our small groups to determine when someone is on the edge.

Our elders have long met every other Wednesday morning for an hour of prayer for the congregation — only that. The other Wednesday we meet in the evening, mostly for business. But we begin with a devotional and then share concerns for the church.

Each week, then, elders have an opportunity to share what they have sensed and seen, and others will either confirm it or mention extenuating circumstances (perhaps the person under discussion simply has been up for two nights with sick children — not a long-term problem). If we agree that someone is under undue stress, after we've shared and prayed about it, we designate a couple of people to spend time with that individual. They will, in turn, offer any help that will better the situation, like arranging a break in the person's church duties.

Three Ways to Maximize Motivation

Naturally, we want to do more than respond to discouragement and burnout. We want to avoid it, or at least minimize it. Our goal is to make the most of people's motivation, to build healthy momentum for outreach.

We have three strategies to do that: spread the load, help people help themselves, and model dependence.

1. Spread the load. If overwork or mismanaged work is causing discouragement, then spreading the work load becomes a logical way to overcome discouragement. Specifically, that means:

● Diversify. Like most churches, we have a number of commissions that do the work of the church. For us, it's five: worship, Christian nurture, fellowship, stewardship, and mission. Our very structure then, assumes that about one-fifth of our time and energy is spent on outreach.

It's easy to understand one of the reasons most churches organize themselves in this way: not everybody can sustain momentum in outreach year after year. Some are not yet ready to do it at all. To give members a variety of avenues of service insures that outreach doesn't overwhelm any individual.

● Give them a break. We not only spread the work load, but also the time load. We'll give people permission to take a break from a ministry, perhaps a year or two, to spend more time with family or to recharge spiritual batteries. The attitude we set is not "This person just couldn't handle the job," but "People have the right and freedom to take a Sabbath rest in ministry." That way people can exit a job without feeling they have to exit the church.

That is easier said than done, of course. About three years ago a young woman bowed out of work because of a health problem. A number of people from the congregation had to encourage her regularly afterward, reminding her that she didn't have to feel guilty about it. If they hadn't done that, she might have quit sharing altogether.

Then again, sometimes the process works cleanly. Recently, a young man released from a responsibility eight months earlier told me how good he felt about it. Once rested, he was anxious to get back to work.

● Know when to say when. Another key to spreading the load is limiting the number of tasks members take on. We don't like to see an average member take on more than two significant jobs at a time. For most people, one is enough.

We have some people, for instance, who participate in our Praise Band. That involves a weekly practice and playing during our Sunday service. Most of these people are also members of a commission, and one or two sit on a board. If they should announce that they want to start an outreach ministry, we'd likely discourage them — unless, of course, they give up another responsibility.

2. Help people help themselves. Since a minister can't be with people in their every ministry situation, it only makes sense to help people help themselves in ministry. In this respect, we do the following.

• Let members do the talking. Members need encouragement not just from their pastor, but from their peers. We let that happen during a time called "Windows of Service." Once a month in worship, we have different individuals talk about how they are sharing Christ's love in their workplace or neighborhood.

About a year ago, the learning center lacked sufficient volunteers. But after a member of the congregation mentioned this during Windows of Service, things were turned around. Since then, the learning center has been owned increasingly by the congregation.

• Enable laity to minister. One of my former associates has been impressed continually at how people stay motivated in our church. I once asked him, "What would you say has been the key to maintaining momentum?"

"More than anything else," he said, "the leadership has been committed to enabling others rather than controlling them." *Enabling* has, of course, become a buzzword in church circles in the last two decades. Let me clarify what I mean by it.

First, it means encouraging others to reach out and evangelize instead of doing it all myself. Not only does this get more ministry done, it also lets members enjoy the wonder of ministry.

Second, enabling means teaming people in the congregation. Experienced people work with those less experienced, but no one is sent out as a lone ranger. Our pastoral team of three is committed to modeling this pattern.

Third, enabling means training people. For example, we run seminars for people who want to help lead worship services. We teach them our theology of worship and how to use language and mannerisms appropriately. We also hold seminars on discipleship in daily life. The point is we try to offer training in areas where our people want and need training to do effective ministry both in and outside the church.

● Support small support groups. Every person needs a sense of achievement, worth, and fulfillment. When people in ministry become independent and cut themselves off from close relationships, they become susceptible to discouragement. They don't have people who can regularly give them encouragement and guidance.

Esther and I belong to a covenant group of thirteen that meets every Thursday evening. Over a six-month period, we take turns sharing with the group our schedules and priorities for the coming months. For instance, when it's my turn, the group discusses how I'm using my time and energy, and how that accords with my gifts. In some areas they encourage me to move ahead, in others, they prompt me to slow down. This group counsel has helped me sort my priorities and it has given me a tremendous sense of freedom to say no to people: "My friends tell me that I'm doing too much and should cut back."

Furthermore, we encourage people to get support from others who participate in similar ministries. For a number of years I have attended three prayer meetings: one with people who minister in the inner city, one with my denominational brothers and sisters, and one composed mostly of suburban pastors. Naturally, there is an altogether different feel and perspective in each group. It's not surprising that the inner-city prayer meeting nourishes me most.

3. Model dependence on God and others. We can prevent discouragement from becoming burnout, but, as I mentioned, we cannot eliminate discouragement. It comes with the territory of a challenging ministry. But we can help people maintain momentum in ministry in the midst of discouragement if we, ourselves, model for them how it is handled. I do that in two settings.

● In small groups. There are some things that pastors need to talk about freely without feeling it's going to be misread or misused in the church. These I don't mention in settings where members are present. Yet I still can talk about a number of things in small-group settings that show people I'm struggling and need their encouragement and prayers.

Esther and I were torn inside when one of our children went through a divorce. During that time, as I sat on the front pew in worship, tears often would run down my cheeks as I asked God for strength to stand up and preach. Of course, our congregation knew what we were going through.

One evening, three people from our congregation came to us and said, "We want to pray with you." We went into my study at the church and prayed. Then they said, "You are carrying all this burden by yourself. We would like you to disengage emotionally for a while. We don't want you even to talk, think, or pray about it for several weeks. We promise you we will do the praying in your place. While we pray daily about this, you unhook."

Their love helped us through our crises. It also helped the congregation see me distraught but accepting their help. If we can practice that type of openness and trust with each other, ministry momentum will be maintained.

● From the pulpit. I think it's wrong for a pastor to say, "Pardon a personal illustration." That's the only kind he really knows. (Actually, it would be more proper to say, "Pardon my borrowing this illustration.")

Although we should remain cautious about using ourselves as illustrations of success, I have fewer qualms about showing people my struggles and God's faithfulness. It is another way of showing that it's normal for people active in ministry to get discouraged, and that we need to depend on God's strength for our momentum.

Purpose and Momentum

Before I was ordained, I volunteered to go to China after college to do relief work. That was in the late 1940s, and I didn't know the Communists were about to take over and close the doors to missionaries. I received a letter from the secretary of missions for my denomination, who knew the situation, telling me I couldn't go, and that surely the Lord would have something for me later in life.

He enclosed in his letter an article by Dick Hillis entitled, "I Was Never Called to China." But Dick had, in fact, been in China for eighteen years. Curious, I read it. He believed he was called to a certain kind of ministry; the location of that ministry, however, was open. If the door closed in one place, he would practice his ministry elsewhere. His ministry wouldn't change, only the locale.

From that day, I've practiced that philosophy. By remembering the purpose of my ministry is to glorify Christ and enhance his kingdom, I stay motivated whatever the place, program, or position. Through disappointments and discouragements, I have yet to lose the wonder.

PART THREE
Strategies

I believe Christians need to be as committed to strategic thinking as they are to prayer, Scripture, and holy living.

— *Frank Tillapaugh*

CHAPTER EIGHT

The Four Spheres of Outreach

Some time ago, the 7-year-old son of an Australian Anglican rector, of whom I was a guest, began to quiz me in his thick "down under" accent. I asked him to repeat a query, thinking I had heard him ask if we had *sex* in our church. Marveling at his precocious curiosity, I was about to reply, "No, we're Baptists," when the light dawned. He was asking if our church had SEBS — the Anglican version of our boys' club program.

Like that little boy, many people tend to think of the church and its ministry in terms of the programs it offers. We do this out of habit: we attend worship, sit on committees, arrange conferences, plan social events. Drifting into comfortable patterns, we give little thought to why we do what we do, let alone whether it's getting us where we want to go.

The church, of course, is more than a set of long-standing programs, but a company of believers who reach out to the world. If the church is to succeed in reaching out, we must invigorate our habitual activities, our "event orientation," with strategic thinking. In fact, I believe Christians need to be as committed to such thinking as they are to prayer, Scripture, and holy living.

More particularly, the kind of thinking I encourage is provoked by two questions: "Who are we trying to reach?" and "What does it take to reach them?"

Strategic Thinking

As I finished leading a seminar on strategic thinking, a businesswoman approached me and said, "We're trying to market our company's products in Asia. Half a day a week, everybody in the company brainstorms. We talk about Japan; we talk about marketing, packaging, advertising. Then we do the same thing with Taiwan, everybody brainstorming what will fit that market." She paused and then asked, "Were you saying that I should be doing that here at my church?"

She had it exactly right! I told her when lay people like her begin to think strategically, then we'll get in touch with the large segments of our culture that daily are growing more alienated from the church.

Pastors can't do this alone. At Bear Valley Baptist Church, we've learned that lay people, who are already immersed in the culture every day, can think strategically about the church's mission if they're guided. The pastors simply instill in people a strategy orientation, give them permission to make ministry decisions, and then get out of the way.

To help us sharpen our strategic thinking, we think about what we call the Four Spheres of Outreach: four cultural categories or spheres of influence that group the unchurched according to their physical and emotional proximity to us. It's a tool that helps us recognize we will contact people in different ways depending on which sphere they are in. Furthermore, it helps us see that each group's lifestyle and circumstances may pose problems that require creative solutions as we reach out.

Sphere One: Fringe Churchgoers

On any Sunday, as many as 25 percent of those attending are what we call *fringe*. Not yet involved in the life of the church, Sphere One people are the unconnected visitors, the occasional church-goers, the "church-hoppers." A church that desires a strong outreach ministry needs to start inside its own walls by reaching these people.

We do that through an enfolding process. This involves three steps: offering a warm welcome, linking newcomers with regulars, and ensuring future contact.

1. A warm welcome. Since a strange place can bewilder a visitor, our first task is to make our church building "user friendly." We don't have all the parking spaces the experts say we need, but we do have well-marked restrooms and a wheel-chair ramp. Our nursery is safe (no sharp corners, carpeted), clean, and well staffed. Windows and a fresh coat of paint enliven an otherwise dark fellowship hall. Even when you don't have spacious facilities, you can take what you have and make it look good and work well.

In addition, our pastoral staff has taken the lead at personally welcoming newcomers. Before we could do so, however, we had to change some traditional pastoral habits. For example, before the Sunday service the pastoral staff normally retreated to the pastor's study to pray. This was by no means a trivial practice, yet strategically, we felt that it cost us our best shot at Sphere One. That fifteen minutes before the service can't be reproduced any other time during the week. It's the only time people come to us. Consequently, our staff agreed to pray and prepare for worship at another time.

Another example is our availability after the service. We felt that the receiving line and mechanical handshake from the preacher sent the wrong message. It encourages people to think of the pastor as the paid performer. Worse, visitors get the same attention every-one else gets. They are forced to take the initiative when what they need is someone, especially the pastor, seeking them out.

We solve these problems with two practices:

— *Do the unexpected.* Mickey Mouse has become my model for the pastor on Sunday morning. At Disneyland, do you ever see Mickey at the gate, greeting people when they enter or leave? Of course not.

Why? Because one of the great laws of communication is: The less anticipated the message, the greater the impact. Kids never know when he's going to pop up; surprise is the secret of his appeal.

One Sunday a visiting seminary professor pulled up outside our church. I happened to be there, so, as I do with other visitors, I opened his car door for him and shook his hand. After that, he called me the "parking lot pastor." He had never seen a pastor in the parking lot. It wasn't anticipated; that's what made an impact on him.

A group of local seminary students went to visit Saddleback Community Church in Southern California, well known for its aggressive visitor program. The students excitedly talked upon their return, not about the sermon or the style of worship, but about the fact that they had been greeted *five times* before they reached the front door.

— *Pastor by walking around.* Tom Peters, in his book, *In Search of Excellence*, talks about "Managing by Walking Around." A good manager, he says, is in casual contact with those he manages. Simi-larly, we need to *pastor* by walking around on Sunday, smiling, laughing, and contacting people informally.

So our staff roams the parking lot, foyer, and pews before and after the service, looking for unfamiliar faces. We don't worry about duplication, because it's important that newcomers are welcomed many times. We introduce ourselves to as many people as possible: "Hi, I'm Frank. How are you doing?" (By the way, I don't introduce myself as the senior pastor. If a newcomer bumps into a friendly character in the foyer who later turns up in the pulpit, I've found they're more receptive to the preaching.)

Consequently, we hear regularly about the different feel at our church: "We met your pastor, and he seems so *normal*." Their questionable judgment aside, that moment with "the guy up front" communicates warmth, an important factor in Sphere One strategy.

2. *Linking people up.* In my contacts, I try to say more than a casual "Hello." I also try to be sensitive. Some people haven't been to church for years or are shy. If I detect discomfort, I back off, tell them I'm glad they're here, and then move on. On the other hand, if they light up at the attention, I weave four questions into our brief conversation:

Where were you born (or raised)?

Where do you live?

Where do you work?

What ages are your kids?

Answers to these help us link newcomers with some person or group in the congregation.

As the visitor answers these questions, I listen for something he or she and a regular attender might share in common. For example, if I greet a young lady who is a nurse and was raised in Texas, and I know of another Texan or a nurse nearby, then I make it a point to introduce them. If I can't do it right then, I note where she sits or which Sunday school class she attends, and point her out to someone in the church. The visitors who feel they have made a connection their first Sunday are far more likely to return.

Naturally, for this strategy to work, I can't spend too much time with any individual. If people seem to need to talk about a problem, I offer an office visit, but ask *them* to call. I tell them I want to give their problem the attention it deserves, but I can't in a crowded foyer just before worship. And, strategically, I leave my Daytimer at home so I can honestly tell them I can't schedule an appointment right now. The key here is to be in control of the conversation, to remember your objectives.

3. *Ensuring future contact.* After Sunday's round of greeting and linking, we arrange follow-up contact. At the staff meeting, we pool our information and scheduling. A home visit or phone call is

best. (We find a letter too impersonal, although it makes a good follow-up to a visit.) A pastor usually makes the first contact, although *who* is not as important as *when* — quickly after people's first visit.

Except in a smaller church, the pastoral staff may take the lead but can't be expected to tackle Sphere One alone. After modeling the enfolding process for a while, we began to train a supplemental group whom we call our Care Core.

On Sundays, they're with us in the parking lot and foyer. During the service, they watch for people who raise their hands for the visitor's brochure, and greet them afterward. Later, Care Core volunteers coordinate follow-up visits and also do hospital calls. Everything is documented and updated in a visitor file, complete with prospect ratings from "good" to "questionable." Our staff and three or four hand-picked Care Core people are enough to handle our average service size of 250.

Sphere Two: Geographically and Relationally Near

Beyond the church doors are people who live or work near the church, have relationships with church members, but are yet to attend a service or event. Anyone in the city that your people know — the Safeway grocery clerk, the skeptical brother-in-law, a co-worker, a next-door neighbor — belong to Sphere Two.

Naturally, these people need to be reached through evangelistic efforts. That means, first, motivating and equipping members to evangelize (which we do with periodic lifestyle-evangelism film series or book studies). But it also means thinking of creative ways to evangelize these people.

The Engle Scale has helped us think about and plan evangelism more wisely. It was developed by James Engle in his book *What's Gone Wrong with the Harvest* and describes thirteen stages of an individual's spiritual development:

-7   Has no awareness of Christianity

-6   Is aware of the existence of Christianity

-5   Has some knowledge of the gospel

-4   Understands the gospel fundamentals

-3   Grasps the personal implications of the gospel

-2   Recognizes a personal need

-1   Repents and professes faith in Christ

 0   Conversion

+1   Evaluates the decision for Christ

+2   Incorporates into a Christian fellowship

+3   Learns and practices the Christian lifestyle

+4   Communes with God

+5   Develops stewardship

+6   Reproduces

With the aid of the Engle Scale, we design our events to give our unchurched friends an appropriate exposure to the Christian faith. Reaching a person who is a -6 or -4 calls for a different tactic than reaching someone in the -3 to -2 range. Our events also lower stress in evangelists as well, because they don't feel personally responsible to take someone from *minus seven* to *plus one* on their own. Instead, over time, their friends can sample slices of the Christian life and, when ready, get an appropriate dose of the gospel. Here, for example, are three different approaches we have tried.

In MOPS (mothers of preschoolers), non-Christian meets Christian while sharing the common joys and pains of raising young children. It's intimate but not threatening, so Christians can invite their -6 and -5 friends. When the need arises, Bible study or a gospel presentation can be introduced. But the program's early-childhood focus binds women together in caring fellowship that naturally results in the sharing of faith.

At Bear Valley we dropped our weekly basketball and softball leagues because they involved relatively few people. In addition, we've learned that it's far easier to get someone to commit to one-day events. So now we periodically hold a sports day. Our first sports day featured multiple events: a volleyball tournament, a softball tournament, and a 10K run. During the day, people clustered around their favorite sport and came together in the evening for an awards program. The day was fun, upbeat, and capped with a local sports personality who spoke about his relationship with Christ.

Adapting Campus Crusade's Executive Outreach program, we staged formal dinners aimed at upscale business and professional people; one dinner was held at a country club and the other at a fine restaurant. At each, Christians sponsored tables, offering non-Christians dinner reservations to hear a notable speaker. The hook was: come hear a business or civic leader share "The Most Important Thing in My Life."

We don't pass the hat at Sphere Two events (remember, stewardship is +5). Our only purpose is to get unchurched people to rub elbows with Christians. Gospel presentations may be direct or indirect, but long-term success is a product of the relationships that grow as lay people befriend the unchurched.

Sphere Three: Geographically Near, Relationally Distant

This sphere comprises people near the church but whom members are not likely to meet daily. Our cities teem with them: the homeless, foreign exchange students, battered children, wheelchair bound veterans, teen-age mothers, elderly shut-ins, crack addicts — all those who can't (or won't) come to us.

Ours is a culture in crisis. Little needs to be done to arouse our awareness of the need; the five o'clock news reminds us about the needs every night. I'm convinced that people want to help but don't know how to get started. Today, upwardly mobile Christians are isolated from these problems. In Sphere One and Two, contact comes easily. In this sphere, however, contact is the main problem, expertise another. We've tackled each problem with a different strategy.

● *Going to the beach.* Newly ordained and already frustrated with the traditional church, Australian pastor John Hurt founded Surf Riders for Christ in 1969. His was the first "parachurch" ministry in Australia. Naturally, the Sydney journalists wondered what prompted a clergyman to start a surfing club. He replied, "If you want to reach surfers, you have to go to the beach." In the same spirit, our strategy is to put Christians into the Sphere Three person's world.

In many cases, contact can be made through existing structures: the halfway house, jail, crisis hotline center, foreign student housing program at the local college. The question is, "How do we get into that system?"

We've found that most systems have what we call a "power broker." In a jail, it's the sheriff. To contact international students, you must work through the campus foreign student adviser. You access the rest home through its activity director.

Once we've found the power broker, we ask, "How do we convince the power broker to let us play on his team?"

A couple at our church called the foreign student adviser at a nearby college, offering to provide host families. The adviser was openly hostile. "You're Baptists! You're just out to evangelize our students." In a calmer moment, she confessed that many of the school's foreign students still were looking for host families. Finally relenting, she agreed to assign several students to us but warned that she would be watching to make sure we didn't force them to attend church or Bible studies.

Then the Iran hostage crisis hit. Most of her sponsoring groups refused Iranian students. After an Iranian shot a teenager who had thrown a brick through his window, the adviser became desperate. At that point, we offered to sponsor her Iranian students, and later we covered their rent and groceries when they stopped getting money from home. Today, she talks about "that wonderful Baptist church" that stuck with her through a tough time. Not only did we reach out to foreign students, but the foreign student adviser, as well.

When we invited the head of Denver Social Services to speak at our evening service, we were straightforward. Our intention was not to force-feed kids on religion, but over time, our commitment to Christ would come out. Did she have a problem with that? Her answer was a striking cultural commentary: "As far as we're concerned, if you're not one of our clients, you're a success. We give you a blank check to model whatever has made you successful. If it's your Christianity, then tell them about it. We don't care. Whatever has kept you out of the social service system will help keep them out." Power brokers aren't looking for Christians per se (and may resist them, at first), but they are motivated to find people who can model positive values.

• *Same skills, new setting.* A common misconception is that, because of the groups we seek to reach, Sphere Three ministry requires special training. On the contrary, we build ministries around the abilities people already possess. We tell people, "Do what you already do, but in a different setting." This helps reduce anxiety, because people see that Sphere Three ministry is realistic and attainable.

People from many backgrounds have responded to the call. A woman from Bear Valley oversees the baby-sitting at our Street School so young mothers can complete their high school studies. She simply transferred her child-care expertise from the suburbs to the inner city. Families that host foreign students need only a willingness to share their home life with a stranger. A physician in our church realized he could make a good living from a half-time medical practice and gives his spare time to a free medical clinic he opened for the poor.

One attorney has taken a dramatic step into Sphere Three ministry. When clients come seeking a divorce, he offers them an intriguing choice. Holding out one hand, he says, "You can put $1000 in this hand, and I'll get you what you're here for." Then he extends the other hand saying, "Or you can put nothing in this hand but *your* hand and listen to some things I'll say, and I'll do everything in my power to reconcile your marriage at no charge." In the last year, ten couples have taken the "free" hand. Five marriages were rescued. Of each of the couples who eventually divorced, at least one partner came to know Christ.

Sphere Three requires immersion in prayer and a group of lay people who have the freedom to fail. It can be a tough assignment and isn't for everybody. But when lay people reach into Sphere Three, crying needs are met, and desperate people are able to meet Christ.

Sphere Four: Geographically and Relationally Distant

This sphere is the concern of what we typically call *missions* — people who are distant and whom we don't know. Like many churches, we encourage our people to consider becoming missionaries in cross-cultural settings.

Bill, for instance, had little time to be involved in the ministries at the church. Having inherited his father's business, he was consumed by the daily grind of running it. His business travels, however, took him to Hong Kong, where he happened to visit some missionaries. By the time he returned, he was transformed. He had been on the front lines of ministry and would no longer be satisfied with a middle-class, "parks and recreation" mentality. One of our leaders invited him down to the City Lights Coffee House. There he saw some of the same kind of front-line ministry he had seen in Hong Kong. So he began to work with the street people there, using some of his wealth to rent a vacant house to start our Street School.

The first step, then, is to give people Sphere Four vision. Getting people to read about mission needs goes a long way toward instilling vision. We've found David Bryant's books, *In the Gap* and *Concerts of Prayer*, especially helpful. They provide a fine overview of the need for mission on our shrinking globe.

In addition, instead of letting mission exposure just happen, as with Bill, we plan short trips to the mission field, because people tend to look at the world differently after such an experience.

Once the vision is created, it's not hard to channel people into Sphere Four ministries. A pastor need only contact a mission organization. Most of them have well-established short-term mission programs and can plug people in. And never in history has travel been easier. William Carey expended an entire year's salary and six months' time getting his family to India in 1793. Today, India is only hours away, and a lot cheaper.

To avoid diluting the resources that might go to the career missionary, we discourage our short-term missionaries from raising support; they usually pay their own way.

We challenge people to invest less money in things and more

in experience. Practically, that means putting off the trip to Disney-land, waiting a year for the Honda Accord, postponing the house hunting.

We also have taken steps to avoid afflicting our missionaries with overly zealous but under-prepared people. Our training of short-term missionaries tries to lower short-termers' expectations.

First, we try to instill a servant attitude. One of the problems that beset early Southern Baptist efforts was short-termer insistence on a Sunday school program in a culture where, especially for adults, the program was offensive. So we warn against setting off for the mission field with an agenda. Their hosts, in fact, likely will ask them to perform menial tasks. One man spent several weeks in Nigeria, sorting cards received from a radio station's listeners. Whether they lay bricks, run errands, or sort cards, their work is affirmed. If they can relieve the career missionaries of tasks that take them away from their main purpose, then they are performing important mission work.

Second, we encourage short-termers to focus on what they *see*, not so much on what they do. Bear Valley's young-singles group sent people to Russia and Mexico City. The choir went to Spain. Others of us traveled to the Philippines. What we saw radically altered how we prayed, used our resources, and spent our time. Cross-cultural missions got the church thinking beyond its walls. That's what we wanted most.

Giving Birth

At Bear Valley, ministries are born, not manufactured. We have a church body that is pregnant with possibilities, and it's the body that is primarily responsible for bringing forth ministries. Though the obstetrician often enjoys prominence, truth to tell, he has little to do with the birth process — all the exciting stuff is happening to the mother! Though our staff initiates a great deal in Sphere One and, to a lesser extent, in Sphere Four, primarily, like the good doctor, our posture is one of relaxed concern. Our job is to encourage, to educate, to assist.

For pastors ready to encourage their church to bear outreach ministries, a good beginning is a small one. We don't recommend a churchwide program implementing the Four Spheres of Outreach. Instead, we suggest working through formal and informal power structures. Sketch it out on a napkin for some key players over breakfast. Talk with the pastoral search committee at the new church. Share one-on-one with staff, elders, and deacons. Ask how they see the church making a difference in each of the four spheres.

First get a core of strategic thinkers committed to outreach; they will eventually impact the formal decision making and can turn event-centered structures inside out.

In the end, a mission-minded church will be born out in the world again, where it belongs.

Effective community outreach requires more than polished techniques. Meaningful outreach begins with a healthy attitude toward mission and the community.
— Myron Augsburger

CHAPTER NINE

Finding Your Church's Niche

A desire to minister to the community doesn't automatically translate into effective community ministry.

A few years ago, an organization was planning a major youth outreach in Washington, D.C. They were going to bring 25,000 young people to Washington and turn them loose to evangelize. Some of us who minister in the inner city met and agreed to send a representative to Chicago to talk with the planning committee. We cautioned them about thrusting thousands of young, white suburban people into an inner-city setting of 70 percent blacks; the cultural barriers are enormous. As a result, they modified the program to develop a more relational approach.

What applies to grand mission projects applies especially to the local church. In approaching our neighborhoods, we don't want to do something foolish or insensitive, but effectively to bring the healing and saving love of Jesus Christ.

Churches that seek to do this begin by asking two fundamental questions: "What should we be doing?" and, equally important, "What should we avoid doing?" Here are principles we've used to help answer those questions. Although our context is the inner city, the principles we use apply to churches in other settings, as well.

Attitude Check

Effective community outreach requires more than polished techniques. Meaningful outreach begins with a healthy attitude toward mission and the community. Here are three attitudes I consider essential.

● *Serve others' needs, not our own.* As we mature in faith, Christians feel increasingly compelled to reach out to others. Sometimes, however, in our efforts to help, we end up merely satisfying our need to serve rather than the community's needs.

Some time ago a young man came to me for advice about becoming an evangelist. (He knew I had worked in interdenominational crusades for twenty-five years.) As we talked, it became evident that he was more driven by his need to do evangelism than an interest in the people who needed Christ. So I recommended that he first become a pastor and get to know and think with a congregation. I felt this would teach him to think first of others' needs, not his own.

Since our church wants to serve people in a way that truly will help them, we think it's important to know firsthand the community to which we minister. Therefore, as I mentioned in Chapter 1, when we started in D.C., I met with other local church leaders. Then I introduced myself to thought makers of the community and joined various community organizations.

When Esther and I moved here, we immediately started getting acquainted with our neighbors. We tried to discover how we could encourage them and what we could learn from them. We not only built bridges of understanding, we also learned about community needs from the people in the community.

When in Tanzania a number of years ago, I read an article by a Roman Catholic missionary from France; it was entitled, "A Stranger in My Father's House." He told how he finally learned to serve people the way they wanted and needed to be served instead of the way he wanted to serve them. That's our goal, as well.

We've also come to see that we cannot serve people without becoming concerned with all of their needs, both spiritual and physical. When we asked the question "How do we carry the love of Christ into our neighborhood?" we've discovered we have to do it with words of witness and deeds of compassion. That is the model Jesus gives us. And it is a necessary model if our evangelistic words are to appear sincere. I don't believe in the old social gospel that reduced the Christian faith to good works. But I do believe in the gospel that meets people's everyday as well as eternal needs.

● *Have a marketplace mentality.* A businessman in a previous congregation I served employed a number of people in his business. After reading Jesus' remarks to the rich young ruler one day, he became troubled. He wondered if he should sell all he had, give it to the poor, and become a day laborer; or should he keep his business, remain a wealthy man, use his wealth to employ people, and serve the community by being a model employer, looking out for the well-being of his workers? In his case, I recommended the latter. So, he began taking a special interest in the children of his employees, arranging scholarships for their schooling, and he offered a profit-sharing plan for his employees.

Sometimes a church cannot offer formal programs that operate out of the church's facilities or are subsidized by church money or personnel. But that doesn't mean the church isn't reaching out to the community. Often, its members are doing so individually and significantly. They initiate and sustain their individual ministries because of the encouragement and strength they receive at church. For example, one successful business executive in our D.C. congregation is a model of stewardship and witness. Although our congregation can't take credit for his faithfulness, he nonetheless is an extension of the church's ministry in the community. In fact, he has asked to be commissioned for his witness in business as others are commissioned for other forms of service.

By broadening our understanding of what constitutes church outreach, we get a better picture of the impact our church is having on the community.

● *Don't dump expertise; offer it.* Esther and I came to Washington, D.C., after spending fifteen years in college administration. Some of our younger alumni who had been working in the inner city told me, "You can't build a three-piece-suit church in inner-city Washington." I answered that I might dress in old clothes and appear to be poor, but as soon as I opened my mouth, it would be obvious that I was educated and privileged. I was going to the inner city, I explained, not to be like the people there or to rescue them heroically. I was going simply because I cared. And because I cared, I would use the benefits of my training, expertise, and experience to help the community as the people there wanted.

The temptation for educated Christians working in poor neighborhoods, however, is to haul out their arsenal of knowledge and expertise to fix the problems. But I've noticed that when I do that, I slap other people in the face with my privilege. On the other hand, to hide my knowledge and connections under a bushel would be selfish; such expertise can help them.

I solve this seeming dilemma by *offering* my expertise and letting the people to whom I minister decide if and when and how they want to use it.

Three Keys to Effective Outreach

If our attitudes must be checked regularly, so must our actions. There are dozens of techniques toward more effective outreach to the community, but three stand out as key.

● *Target the right community.* There are three "cities" in Washington, D.C.: First, the federal government, made up of the people who work in the offices of Congress, the White House, the cabinet departments, and other federal agencies. Second, the several thousand business people who commute to the city during the day. Third, the Washington, D.C., from six o'clock in the evening until six in the morning, composed of the people who struggle to survive in the confines of the official city limits. Each of these cities has its own network and interacts only sporadically with the other two Washingtons.

We had to decide which "city" we were going to minister to. In our case, located as we are in the inner city, it was not a difficult choice. We chose to reach out to those who live and work in the city, not primarily the daytime commuters or ever-changing federal government work force.

Having chosen, we now can focus our energies and intelligently evaluate our work. When people ask, "Are you making an impact on Washington, D.C.?" we don't have to apologize for not getting more bills passed in Congress, or for not having senators join our congregation. That has not been our target community. Instead, we talk about our work in the inner city and the community being formed among young professionals.

● *Allow outreach programs to trickle up.* We have a learning center with ten computers, and about forty neighborhood children come to use them every week. The learning center evolved from the vision of one of our church members. She and her husband, in watching the children of the area, began thinking about how they could be tutored. First, they enlisted people from our church who would be willing to tutor the children. Then, they went to the local school and asked for a list of the underachievers and started tutoring them evenings at the church. When these underachievers started achieving, the demand increased. At that point, a businessman gave us twenty thousand dollars. With it we bought computers, which we use with the students.

I could cite another half-dozen illustrations of other programs of our church that were started by concerned church members who felt called to meet a particular need. They formed groups to focus on a concern and then took steps to meet the need. That's a process we encourage. In fact, only then will the congregational boards (elders and deacons) become involved.

Many churches, instead, wait for the administrative body to

act first. Committees are assigned to carry out something the board has decided should be done. Or the pastor tells the congregation the six or seven things they ought to be doing in the community. Time and again, such projects go nowhere. That's because (1) the people have no ownership of the projects, and (2) the ideas, often generated by those away from the front lines, may not meet the needs of the people they seek to reach.

Consequently, our elders don't initiate outreach programs. Our usual pattern is to pray and wait for a concern to emerge from a group in the church. One person with a burden is not enough. But when others begin to show an interest in that ministry, the elders encourage them to develop a plan, recruit the people needed, and launch the ministry.

When I was commissioned to start our congregation, the secretary of the board with which I worked said, "Myron, you'll need to let the body of Christ that emerges in Washington determine its own character." That is exactly what we're trying to do.

● *Know thyself.* A church that sincerely seeks to meet community needs is faced with a unique temptation: to do too much.

Sometimes, even when a group has banded together for a particular ministry, we don't give them the go-ahead, even if the need is pressing. We're concerned about becoming overextended and ineffective. Sometimes, we simply don't have the funds to support the group's ideas. At other times, we're not sure we can staff a project over the long run.

For example, we've put our desire for a youth coffee house on hold. It would be designed for young people in both the church and neighborhood. It would be a safe place for them to gather on Friday, Saturday, and Sunday evenings. If designed well (neon lights, nice furnishings) and adequately staffed, it would be popular and meet a community need. We've gone so far as to check out facilities and locations. But if we took on the project now, we could not give it our best effort. We would end up with an inadequate facility and a poorly staffed, poorly funded ministry. We and the community can do without that.

We also have dreams about creating a dentistry clinic, a counseling center, and a legal clinic. All in good time, I trust. But as much as a church wants to help, sometimes it's better to say no for a while.

Some people, of course, confront us because we're not doing something for them. I don't like to hear that type of criticism. But if our church is genuinely doing what it can, I can challenge the critic confidently.

One evening a young man came to my office. He accused me and the church of being racists. "If you were sincere about your religion," he said, "you would . . ." and he produced a list of both personal and political demands.

When I could swallow no more, I said, "I've listened to you. Now I want you to listen to me." After explaining to him why I was ministering in the inner city and what the church was doing, I said, "You don't know me or this church or what we're about. I wouldn't have moved into this black community if I were a racist." I suggested he forget the racist rhetoric and open his eyes to who his real friends are.

He didn't know what to say, but finally he said, "You've got black blood in you or you wouldn't understand me like that. I don't know how much, but you've got some black blood."

"Come off it," I said. "Cut me. Cut yourself. It's the same color blood. This isn't about race, but caring."

So, every time the community says, "Jump!" the church shouldn't ask, "How high?" If it is sincerely reaching out to the community in some ways, it can say no to things it can't do well.

The Pastor's Role: Prod and Praise

If commitment to a mission project arises from the congregation, it doesn't happen automatically. As a pastor, I am not able to do all of the outreach, but I am one of the main people who encourages it. There are three of us on the pastoral team who consider ourselves enablers of the congregation.

Preaching is an integral part of the process of finding a church's niche in the community. It's not that I tell our people what they should be doing — "Open a food closet!" or "Establish a drug clinic!" Instead, I try to present God's Word and speak about the community in such a way that people begin to ask, "What should we be doing for Christ in this community?"

Second, I encourage people by pointing them in the right direction. When people or groups come to me with an idea for outreach, we help them find resources, encourage them, and pray with them.

Third, as a pastor, I give public support to outreach ministries. There are dozens of ways of doing this without dominating the process. For example, the pastors don't give announcements about the progress or needs of a particular ministry; it's much better if that sort of thing comes from the people involved in the ministry itself. But following the announcement, I will thank the person for the presentation and affirm the project. It helps the congregation support a project if their pastor supports it.

When and How to Work with Caesar

Sometimes as a church ministers to its community, it will run into government. Either the government is not adequately providing justice as it should (civil rights is the classic example), or the church needs the government's help to provide a service (e.g., permits and/or funds needed to open up a food closet). In either case, the church has to work with the governing authorities to meet a human need. But how do we do that effectively?

Naturally, a great deal of the answer depends on one's theology of church and state. Yet there are some practical principles we've found helpful that most Christians can agree on.

First, the church does not serve the state; we serve Jesus Christ. Therefore, we are not going to compromise our ethics or principles just to get a few dollars. The dollars aren't as important as our integrity. I've seen groups expend great effort to get a grant and then have the shape of their program determined by that grant. Some are tempted to do unethical things to manipulate the source of funds to their ends.

We recently received permits to renovate a building for the Christian College Coalition, but only after countless delays and red tape. Some of our people speculated that a little payola would have greased the wheels of the bureaucracy. We know that other organizations have walked their projects through without the problems we encountered, but they may have made sure "a certain expense was covered," which helped in processing the permit. There may have been other reasons for our delays, but the fact that we didn't play this game may have been one. In the end, it cost us a great deal of time, but we maintained the integrity of our ministry.

Second, we can develop relationships and encourage dialogue with people with political power. Our temptation is to depersonalize government with labels and titles, to distance ourselves and stand back in judgment. But government is made up of people, and the better we know these people, the better we understand the constraints with which they live. And the better they know us, the more genuine our interchange becomes. As I've gotten to know some of these individuals, I've come to realize many people in government struggle to do what's right. So, I don't criticize them carelessly.

Third, sometimes we do need to confront officials. We hold convictions on justice and peace that sometimes compel us to speak. But when I confront officials, I don't necessarily do it to get the state to do what I want. I simply want the government to honor and respect the consciences of those who hold different views.

As a pacifist I was opposed to the war in Vietnam. Yet while the war raged on, I didn't write angry letters or publicly denounce the government. But along with seven others, I did visit senators and Secretary of State Henry Kissinger to tell them our views about war. We made no impassioned speeches; we simply explained our position and quoted some passages from Scripture. We wanted them and President Nixon, who were talking about "peace with honor" at the time, to see that there was a higher honor yet. We also tried to show them that we spoke for a good number of the governed they represented.

We were not trying to create a pacifist government; the government has a right to have an army and protect its shores. But if our government is to be a government of all the people, it needs to understand the convictions of all of its people.

Some Seeds Fall on Good Ground

In our outreach ministries we often don't see the results of our efforts. We don't know what has happened to the family of six that came to the food closet last month. We don't always know what pregnant teenagers finally decide. And sometimes we're tempted to give up because we see the needy taking advantage of the church's kindness.

It helps me, in such times, to remember the example of our Lord, who gave with no thought of return. I also remember that much of ministry is merely planting seeds. As in Jesus' parable, some are going to fall on stony ground, and some will grow among weeds, but the sower continues to sow. Every once in a while, we see the seed sprout and grow and bear fruit. And that reminds me that God, indeed, is at work in our congregation.

A man came by the church building one evening just as I was ready to leave. He said he had just gotten out of prison and didn't have any place to stay, nor any money. He didn't want to go, as he put it, "knock somebody off" again to get what he needed. So I talked with him about his deepest needs. I told him about Christ, and we prayed together. Then I called a friend at the Union Rescue Mission to get him a room for the night. Finally, I handed him a five dollar bill and told him how to take the bus to the Rescue Mission. He looked at me in amazement and said, "You're going to see me Sunday morning."

Well, Sunday morning came and he didn't show up. The next Sunday he wasn't there, either. Six weeks went by with no contact from him.

Then one afternoon a knock came on the church door. As I opened it, my eyes fell on a man dressed neatly in a suit, a Tiparillo dangling from his mouth. He was the man I gave the five dollars to six weeks earlier.

"Preacher," he said, "I've gotta talk with you." He came in, bubbling with excitement. "I want to tell you that Man-Up-There is as good as you said he is." He told me all about the job he had gotten. Then he said, "Tell me how to open a savings account. I'd like to get a car. And I'd like to get married someday, and . . ." I smiled as he rattled off his new dreams.

I see him from time to time on the street, and he is still doing well, still dreaming great dreams. Of course, he has a way to go. I'd like to see his faith blossom, for instance. But I remain hopeful. And I continue to cast seeds of the gospel his way when I see him. Who knows when and where God will cause that seed to bear more fruit?

Pastors, particularly in these times of volatile change and complex situations, can help lay a foundation for effective outreach by establishing that, for the most part, methods are "up for grabs" in the church. We will encourage any honorable means to reach people for Christ.

— Frank Tillapaugh

CHAPTER TEN

Encouraging Target-Group Outreach

We all want to reach the unchurched with the gospel, but most people who need Christ are not going to walk through the church doors, no matter how widely we open them, no matter how great our Sunday school, no matter how well-planned our worship service. That's where target groups come in. Target-group outreach enables a church to touch the people who would not otherwise be exposed to the gospel.

A target group is simply people who share a common need or experience on whom the church focuses its outreach. Instead of broadly scattering the gospel to all "people without Christ," target-group ministry aims its sights on one particular group of people with specific needs. If mass evangelism is like watering a garden with a sprinkler (which may waste some water and may not give each plant the exact amount of water it needs), target-group evangelism is like watering each plant with a hose (which not only saves water but attends to the specific needs of each plant).

Target-group ministry usually springs up when someone recognizes a need no one else is meeting adequately. This happened, for instance, in a church located between territories of the Bloods and Crips, gangs in the Watts area of Los Angeles. At times, as the gangs battled over turf, the neighborhood became a war zone. A 12-year-old girl from the church was the victim of a drive-by shooting. A stray bullet ripped through a window in her home, struck her in the head, and killed her.

In response to this tragedy, her parents moved from grief to action: they started praying with other parents for the protection of their children. Eventually they created a ministry called KOYA — Keep Our Youth Alive. They contacted local police for advice on effectively dealing with gang violence. They began discussing the best ways to improve the safety of their neighborhood. Soon unchurched families troubled by gang violence became involved and were pointed to Christ as these church people addressed their needs.

Then the parents learned that when police officers find gang members, they often discover 8- to 12-year-old "jeopardy kids" tagging along — kids in the pipeline to gang membership. So the parents began working with the Los Angeles Police Department to create a separate group to provide these children alternatives to gang membership — sports, big-brother and big-sister programs, and financial bonuses for staying in school. Out of one experience, then, two target groups were identified.

A group of church people recognized the needs of a special group — some churched, some unchurched — and by dealing with the need, they exposed the unchurched to the faith and works of the church. That is target-group evangelism.

The Targets Are Multiplying

When I came to Bear Valley Baptist Church in 1971, I began talking about target-group evangelism immediately. It took six years simply to develop the mind-set. We didn't start a target-group ministry until 1977. But then several groups started at almost the same time — ministries to international students, singles, and street people.

Later, other ministries emerged to such target groups as unwed mothers, seniors, alcoholics, and mothers of preschoolers. Today, the number of groups churches are targeting is multiplying.

How do we become aware of the needs? In many cases, the media help us by identifying needy groups: the illiterate, the homeless, victims of abuse, AIDS patients, parents of runaways. In a few years, no doubt, we'll be ministering to target groups that we're unaware of today.

The diversity of groups desperately needing God's grace seem to be expanding exponentially. Are these people reachable in the traditional church structure? In many cases, probably not. If we are going to bring the gospel to these people, we'll need to find creative approaches. Target-group strategy frees people to do that.

Because of their varied origins, target groups do not have strict parameters in regard to size, scope or focus. They can consist of a few members reaching out to street people, a small group of professionals establishing a health-care clinic in the inner city, or a whole network of members providing day-to-day care and support for unwed mothers.

The methods and means will differ, but we've discovered several principles are strategic in making target-group ministry work.

What Pastors Can Do

The pastor's main role is to develop a conducive atmosphere where target groups can spring up and flourish. Here are four ways I've tried to do that.

1. Focus on our freedom to create new ministries. Not only do I preach about the importance of outreach, I show the wide variety of means Christians have used.

I've told the congregation, "I find it significant that while the Bible deals extensively with the content of the gospel, it is silent about the techniques and structures of evangelism. We have an absolute and transcendent message, but Scripture seems to leave our methods more open than we sometimes think."

The early church left us few records of its methodology. We have only a handful of clues about how those first groups worked things out. We know churches had elders and deacons, that apostles were sent out to preach and start churches, and that many were won by the example of Christian love. But we aren't given "The Biblical Strategy" to reach the world.

Our people have been freed when they realize no policy manual has to be memorized. No one says a target group *must* meet weekly or that they *must* take minutes of their meetings or *must* hold elections. Those decisions are left up to them.

Pastors, particularly in these times of volatile change and complex situations, can help lay a foundation for effective outreach by establishing that, for the most part, methods are "up for grabs" in the church. We will encourage any honorable means to reach people for Christ. At times this will require the wisdom and oversight of the church board, as was the case when our singles ministry wanted to sponsor dances. For our Baptist church, that caused spirited, though healthy, discussion.

But the point is: nearly any method is open for consideration, even if we have to give it a hard look.

2. Give visibility to target groups. Pastors also can point people in the right direction and cheer them on. We can use target groups as positive illustrations in sermons and talk about their importance in informal conversations.

Throughout the year, we highlight every target ministry, giving the group leader three or four minutes during worship to explain the ministry.

We also run a "Did You Know" section in the weekly bulletin to alert our congregation to the needs of various groups. One member, who treats this as her ministry, canvasses all the target ministry leaders on what they would like to include in "Did You Know." Perhaps the ministry to unwed mothers needs cribs, or the prison ministry is seeking a teacher on Tuesday nights, or the seniors are hosting a special lunch. This helps keep the church informed.

Our annual Celebration Sunday also becomes an opportunity to introduce all target-group ministries to the church. Some provide short slide shows describing their work and mission.

Of course, each target group needs plenty of publicity and is tempted to overuse pulpit opportunities. So we've limited the amount of time we spend giving announcements about target groups' activities. In fact, our target ministries are allowed but one pulpit announcement when they are beginning. Following that kick-off promotion, they can make use of church bulletins, newsletters, or Sunday school time, but they understand we must restrict pulpit access.

At times, we have featured a Ministry of the Month. We briefly mention it during the service and set up a booth or table in the foyer where information and materials are distributed. All this helps get information out, without shortcutting the time allotted to teaching, preaching, and worship.

3. Support target-group leaders. Beyond giving visibility, we also need to provide a support system for target-group leaders. Sustaining these key people is an important function, and making sure those support systems are in place is one of the things a pastor can do. For instance, I recommend at least quarterly meetings for target-group leaders, one of them being an overnight retreat where they can support one another in collegial fashion. In addition, they also can look back over the past year and present their goals and vision for the coming year.

Target-group leaders usually lament their failures rather than recognize their successes. Their reports are often apologetic: "We could do better" and "We could use more help." The refrain is almost universal. But the rest of the group helps the leaders focus on the good their ministry is doing. And my role, as pastor, is to keep reminding them that they are called first to be faithful. A ministry will ebb and flow, and periods of unusual success usually come only after failure and static times.

Sometimes cross-pollination between target-group leaders solves specific problems. The leaders of our unwed mothers' ministry, for instance, shared with the group that they were concerned about their ability to offer child care for the new moms who were taking classes. It so happened that our street school had a child-care ministry already in place. They offered the service to the moms, as well. Problem solved.

4. Keep the climate safe and positive. Nothing destroys a healthy atmosphere faster than allowing target groups to use guilt for promotional purposes. We make it clear that no group is more important than another. No one is allowed to place "monkeys" on other people's backs.

This means that I, as pastor, must be careful not to suggest that people give special allegiance to activities I'm involved in.

It also means that I explain from the pulpit: "If anyone comes up to me and says, 'Pastor, our church ought to be doing such and such,' I'm going to say, 'Obviously the Holy Spirit has given you a special concern about this, and that probably means it's up to you to do something about it.' I try to be sensitive to what the Holy Spirit wants me to do, but I can't possibly change my focus every time someone says, 'Pastor, you should be responsible for this.' So don't feel guilty for not joining every ministry. We'll be offering you lots of opportunities to serve. Find what God wants you to do, and do it!"

When people understand these ground rules, a weight comes off. It's like parenthood: most parents feel a little guilty at times because none of us thinks we've done a good enough job with our kids. Likewise many church people feel guilty because they aren't doing "enough."

As pastor, I want to provide principles that relieve people of inappropriate, undeserved guilt and help them identify where they can contribute joyfully. I want to do more than run successful programs. I also try to create an atmosphere in which people can recognize needs and do something significant to meet them.

5. Provide guidelines for freedom and responsibility. Pastors can

also encourage target-group ministry by establishing clear bound-
aries. When people understand the expectations, they are free to be
creative within them. At Bear Valley we have four simple guidelines, which have helped us launch healthy target groups.

• Don't ask for money. Waiting for funding from the church
budget is a leading killer of good target-group ministry ideas. Not
only does the ministry die before it's been born, but so does the
enthusiasm and creativity of the people eager to get started. That's
why we aim to penetrate a particular subculture with an effective
target ministry without depending on church funds. Why let a tight
budget (and what budget isn't?) prevent ministry from happening?

So, if not the church budget, how do we finance these new
ministries? Here's how one of our target ministries creatively did it.

Ten years ago, some of our women wanted to minister to
unwed mothers. The only such ministry they knew involved group
homes where unwed mothers lived prior to giving birth. These
operations required facilities, full-time staff, and substantial funding. Eventually, they began exploring ways to do this without substantial funding. They decided to invite these women into private
homes rather than an institutional setting. The group sought out
church couples with strong marriages and an extra bedroom who
could handle the housing and support of an unwed mother until the
birth of the baby. This not only made financial sense, it gave the
unwed mother family care and the couple an opportunity for ministry in their home.

Since the inception of this ministry, we have directly housed
or provided support for almost two hundred women. And it has
been done with no budget other than the time and resources of a
group of caring people.

• Run the ministry in its entirety. When leaders step down,
the responsibility to replace them lies with the group. Since our
church staff does not attempt to direct the individual groups on a
day-to-day basis, the task of recruiting new members is best left to
the group itself.

• Stay out of moral trouble. We let our target-group leaders
know that they are expected to remain above reproach in their

personal lives.

● Stay out of doctrinal trouble. Likewise, our target-group leaders know that their ministries must remain consistent with the biblical and doctrinal stance of the church. If one of our target groups would begin to champion a theological issue that differs from the church's position, the church leaders would step in.

What a Pastor Doesn't Do

While a pastor can play an important role in creating a climate conducive to healthy target-group evangelism, there are a couple of things I, as a pastor, definitely do *not* do.

First, as pastor, I do not assume responsibility for solving difficulties the group faces. No matter how tempted I am to step in and dictate a solution, it's a better strategy to allow groups to resolve their own problems.

Our ministry to people involved in cults illustrates this point. The cults ministry was started by a strong, aggressive individual who targeted Jehovah's Witnesses and Mormons for door-to-door evangelism. He and his team would attend events sponsored by various cults to pass out Christian pamphlets.

When the leader moved away, the rest of the group didn't know what to do. They asked the pastors to provide leadership. After meeting with them and discovering they wanted more than our moral support, I explained that the pastoral staff couldn't rescue them.

Some of the team members got angry: "Don't you care about this ministry?" Yes, we did. But the resolution of their problems rested within the group. As pastors, we honestly didn't have the time or resources to get involved. And if we did, it would create a dependence, which could loom large in the future. So despite the discomfort, both for the pastors and the group, we placed responsibility back on the group.

For a while the group languished; at times the members doubted they would continue. Eventually, however, one group member discovered that more Baptists enter cults than do members of any other denomination (probably because there are more of us

Baptists), and that stirred the group's imagination. They shifted their strategy from aggressive evangelism to education geared at stopping the flow of Baptists into cults. They enlisted former cult members who had come to know Christ and put together an excellent seminar. They presented it on Sunday evenings and in Sunday schools.

The group went through three phases: aggressive outreach, languishing, and educational ministry. Even though I preferred their initial approach, during their time of rethinking I left the decisions to them. If I'm not playing the game, I don't call the plays. They needed a strategy based not on *my* interests, but on the *group's* interests. They came out of that period having developed their own solutions and a ministry in which they could invest themselves.

This leads to the second thing pastors are *not* to do in target-group ministry: insist that groups meet certain standards of effectiveness. We all want to see successful ministries, and our temptation, when we see target-group ministries that are limping along ineffectively, is to step in and upgrade the program or terminate it.

The problem with stepping in, of course, is the expectation you create. And what happens when you have twenty target groups and each wants pastoral leadership? You can't possibly give each the attention it needs.

The problem with terminating a faltering ministry is that many times success is built on the rubble of numerous failures. Healthy ministries usually have gone through a period of ineffectiveness before they ultimately emerge stronger and more effective. Often we see a ministry struggle and when given breathing room, turn things around with no outside help.

The key to accommodating target-group ministries successfully is to live with "relaxed concern." I'm not callous; I remain concerned. But if God isn't initiating a specific work in people's hearts, I can and should relax.

Common Problems in Target-Group Ministry

Even though I'm sold on the value of target-group outreach, the strategy presents problems. Here are some of the difficulties and the adjustments we've made.

1. Church members can be uncomfortable with people "unlike us." In the late seventies, our church sponsored a recovered homosexual and his wife. We housed them in a home we ran for street people, and they worked in our inner-city ministry of street witnessing. They also spent a few evenings a week in Denver's gay bars, sharing the gospel, inviting people to the Genesis Center and to our church.

One Sunday I mentioned from the pulpit, "We have another street ministry at the Genesis Center, and one of their targets is Denver's homosexuals." After I said it, I could feel the fear ripple through the church: *Oh my goodness, these people will be coming to our church!*

Fortunately, at Bear Valley our strategy includes multiple congregations. We offer a variety of worship services and times. The people from the street ministry gravitated to the 5:45 P.M. Sunday service, which was less frequented by the typical, mainstream congregation members. Everyone seemed to be comfortable as a result.

But the larger question is how to assimilate people who are different. The problem of assimilation needs to be addressed from the outset of any target ministry. If a ministry is started, we assume those leading the ministry are also concerned with the problem of getting those people plugged into the life of our church. We expect these target-group leaders to develop their own strategies for incorporating people from their ministries into the life of the church.

2. Some target-group ministries are risky. In our litigious society, some target-group ministries bring with them the threat of lawsuits. Because of the possibility of accidents, violence, or emotional opposition, we have organized our riskier ministries under a separate legal umbrella, Bear Valley Ministries, Inc.

If a target-group ministry has a paid staff, if it has its own facilities, or if its activities create greater risk, then we place it under the second corporation. With paid staff, there is a greater chance of being sued than with a purely volunteer program. Our coffee house in downtown Denver fits this category. We have a pastor working in the neighborhood with street people, and we feel it's wise to have the ministry under a separate board of directors and to have liability insurance to cover all the activities.

We operate our cult ministry under this arrangement, too — even though the staff is unpaid — because it's a controversial and emotionally charged area. We also placed our wilderness camping ministry, Peak Adventures, under this umbrella because of the risks in backpacking and rock climbing. So far we have not had any problems with lawsuits over slander or personal injury, but we have seen other churches face legal proceedings because of such charges.

In our situation, this is the best solution for potential lawsuits. Naturally, every church will want to confer with its attorneys about its community and state laws to determine the best way to handle this threat locally.

3. Traditional ministries may feel target ministries are competition. Early in our experience with target groups, I made the mistake of pushing too hard to create a mind-set for target groups. For me, it was easy to become enamored with new ministries while taking older, foundational ministries (choir, Sunday schools, nursery) for granted. My sermon illustrations and my casual conversation tended to focus on the target groups. People wondered if I valued the children's choir as much as the ministry to unwed mothers.

I quickly realized my error. Now I work hard to maintain balance. We try to give our target-group ministries and the more traditional, mainstream ministries equal emphasis from the pulpit and in our publicity.

4. Neglecting part of the gospel. In the past, our people have launched target-group ministries because they longed to save people's souls. As the ministry develops, however, people become more concerned about meeting physical and emotional needs, and less about the spiritual. As pastor, my goal is to see both elements balanced in a whole-person emphasis.

Consequently, from the pulpit, in Sunday school presentations, at church meetings, through newsletters, and in conversations with ministry leaders, we talk about how we can bring "the whole gospel to the whole person." We stress that we have good news for every facet of life.

In addition, I regularly ask target-group ministry leaders: "Are you including the whole gospel in your message?" or "Are you addressing the whole person with your ministry?"

The whole-gospel/whole-person concept is not difficult to communicate, but it must be addressed constantly as ministries mature. We cannot afford to lose sight of our evangelical purpose and mission by focusing on meeting physical needs. The message of God is good news for every dimension of life.

Ongoing Results

Target groups are effective. They provide a manageable way for Christians to meet the physical and spiritual needs of a specific group of people. The measure of success is not whether we have two or twenty or two hundred target groups. The question is whether we are offering the gospel to people in a way they can understand and appreciate.

I talked not long ago with some of the people who work with inner-city children in our street school ministry. This program offers kids who have dropped out of school a full-fledged junior high and senior high curriculum; they can earn not just a GED, but a high school diploma. The Marine Corps has been referring some potential recruits, who lack high school credentials, to this program.

Recently, nine students graduated, and three of them were entering the Marines. These students had gotten their diplomas, but some of them also had been introduced to Jesus Christ and prepared to live as Christians in the military.

To me, that's success: nine kids had a need, we were able to help them meet it, and in the process they were introduced to Jesus. That's target-group ministry at its best.

I remain committed to evangelistic preaching, not just because of the Great Commission, but also because of its great satisfaction.

— *Myron Augsburger*

CHAPTER ELEVEN

Preaching Evangelistically

Since day one, the church has used one method to reach out to people more frequently and more successfully than any other. It's the way the gospel was brought to Europe by Paul, and the way it spread throughout the West by the Dominican and Franciscan orders, among others. It was central in the life, worship, and outreach of the Reformation. It was the means by which lives were ignited and entire towns transformed in the great awakenings in this country. Today, it remains the one task, more than any other, that most congregations expect of their pastors, because it is the main vehicle for communicating to them and the larger community God's grace and peace. I'm talking, of course, about preaching.

A church can and should reach out to the community in a variety of ways, many of which are discussed in this book. But we would be remiss if we overlooked preaching, particularly evangelistic preaching. All preaching seeks to communicate God's grace and peace, but evangelistic preaching is unique. In that sense, it deserves particular attention.

Objections to Evangelistic Preaching

In spite of its noble history, some preachers remain hesitant about evangelistic preaching. Many wonder about the place of the evangelistic sermon in a church setting, where the hearers supposedly are already believers. The four objections I encounter most, and my responses, are these:

• *Evangelistic sermons don't help believers.* Since evangelism is aimed at the unbeliever, and since unbelievers usually constitute only a small minority of a congregation, some preachers reason that the evangelistic sermon is out of place in worship. Not quite. In spite of these assumptions, the evangelistic sermon remains necessary also for the believer, for three reasons.

First, it helps believers clarify how they will present the gospel to their friends during the week. When they hear the pastor articulate the evangelistic message, it gives them a model and a message for their own witnessing. Frequently members thank me for a sermon that gave them ways to explain their faith to a friend at work.

Second, the evangelistic sermon gives relatively nonverbal members an opportunity to share the gospel with their friends, without saying a word! Many of our members bring friends to church so they not only can see the gospel at work, but also hear it articulated. Once, a Sunday school class invited their unchurched friends to a dinner, and they clarified on the invitation that a pastor would be present to talk about Christ. My presence as a pastor offered a natural way to introduce Christ into the evening.

Third, people who regularly come to church don't necessarily have a personal relationship with Christ and, thus, need to be evangelized — to hear and respond to the Good News.

A number of years ago, Archbishop William Temple formed a commission to study evangelism in England. The commission concluded that the church is a field for evangelism when it ought to be a force for evangelism. It has also been estimated by Elton Trueblood that two-thirds of the members of the American churches know nothing about personal conversion. We may disagree about the numbers, but few pastors will deny the reality.

I once preached at a noonday service in which struggling single parents were being ministered to, both with preaching and with gifts of food and clothing. After the service, as people were filing out, shaking my hand, one woman, well dressed and dignified, said, "Thanks for that message. That was just what they needed."

I held onto her hand and said, "But don't we all need it?"

"Well, maybe sometime I'll be in trouble," she replied, "and then I'll need it."

"Are you married?" I asked. She acknowledged she was. So to make a point I said, "I guess you needed a man in your life. Is that why you got married?"

She stiffened. "I love my husband. *That's* why I married!"

"Well, that's the way it is with salvation," I said. "It isn't a crutch we use because we're in trouble. We walk with Christ because we love him."

Those who have never known Christ personally and those whose relationship has become stale need to hear the Good News presented afresh.

● *Evangelistic sermons are simplistic.* Some preachers think their preaching gifts and their congregations demand sermons that challenge the mind. They assume the evangelistic sermon does anything but that, because it aims at people's most elementary need. They are right about the aim of the sermon, but they couldn't be more wrong about its intellectual quality.

An evangelistic sermon will clarify the gospel and highlight its uniqueness in the world today. That means, then, the preacher must understand clearly the alternatives to Christ, many of which are world views that listeners hold. In addition, the preacher will have to work at speaking fairly about these other views, for listeners will turn off the one who sounds uninformed or biased.

To put it another way, if you're trying to communicate the gospel in the midst of the modern world, when New Age, existentialist, hedonist, and materialist world views compete for people's loyalties, you can be sure evangelistic preaching will challenge preacher and listener intellectually.

Not that we need to sound academic. In fact, we shouldn't. But that makes the task even more challenging. Although we must recognize the complexity of world views people hold, and the complexity of reasons for holding them, we need to translate Christian theology into the clearest and simplest language.

I was invited to speak at a week-long, city-wide crusade in Salt Lake City in 1963. Early in the week, a spokesman for the Mormon church went on television and said, "Go to this meeting. We need a revival of religion in America. It'll do you good. But remember, we've got all this and more." I felt my task was to show that they didn't have all this, let alone more.

On the first night I spoke on Hebrews 1, that passage that highlights the uniqueness of Christ so eloquently. In short, the text and the situation demanded that I speak on Christology. But I also needed to communicate the uniqueness of the church's Christology in ways people could understand.

So, I said plainly that Jesus is not a prophet in a series of prophets. In that setting, they knew exactly what I meant. Then I explained that Christians do not say Jesus is like God, as many do when they speak about their prophet, but that God is like Jesus:

"If my son walked in and said, 'I'm John Myron Augsburger, Myron Augsburger's son,' people might say, 'Well, of course. You're like your father.' But if they hadn't seen me and they met him, they couldn't say that; they wouldn't have any comparison to make. But they could say, 'Ah! So this is what the Myron Augsburger family is like.' "

I concluded by explaining that no other person or prophet is like Jesus, because he is the only one who expresses to us what the

Father is like.

Competent evangelistic preaching can be more formidable than giving a lecture in a seminary classroom. Not all evangelistic preaching will be intellectually demanding. But if we want to challenge people to love God with their minds, much of it will be.

• *Evangelistic preaching is event oriented.* Some evangelistic preachers simply aim to bring listeners to the edge of decision and then go for the jugular at the invitation, using any tactic available. Naturally, some church members hesitate to bring friends to hear such a presentation, fearing the tactics used by the evangelist will alienate their loved ones and put a strain on those relationships.

If that's evangelistic preaching, it's understandable that many pastors want nothing to do with it. Neither do I. Yet I don't abandon evangelism in the pulpit.

Instead, I do it differently. When evangelistic preaching becomes merely event oriented, it becomes unlike the rest of the Christian life, which is a long-term proposition. That's why I take the long view when I preach evangelistically.

When I preach as an evangelist, I recognize that people may have invited friends. Some people present may not know Jesus Christ in a personal way, and some Christians present have ongoing relationships with these unbelievers. My goal is to enhance that relationship by pointing the unbeliever to Jesus, not damage that relationship.

I was scheduled to preach evangelistically in British Columbia earlier this year. The organizers and I agreed to have a session for educators. The idea was to encourage the Christian school teacher to invite an unbelieving colleague to a dinner meeting where the Christian message would be presented.

In that setting, then, through preaching and discussion that followed, I aimed to interpret why Christianity makes sense out of life. And when I was through, I wanted the Christian school teacher to remain comfortable driving home with the unbelieving colleague he or she invited. So, I tried to present the claims of Christ compellingly but leave people the freedom to think and reflect about their decision. That means I must trust the Holy Spirit to work in people's lives over time, as he always does.

● *Evangelistic preaching depends on the preacher*. Some preachers quail before the evangelistic sermon. They look at their preaching gifts and the awesomeness of the evangelistic task, and they refuse to do it from the pulpit. There's too much riding on the sermon, they feel, and they don't think they're up to the task.

Well, less rides on the preacher than they think. Naturally, preachers do well to craft their message so that it presents the Good News in as compelling a fashion as possible. But we also do well to remember that the effectiveness of evangelistic preaching depends in great part not on us but on the members of the church.

Billy Graham came to Washington, D.C., a few years ago to lead a crusade. As usual, thousands attended, and many became Christians, including a few people connected with our church.

One young woman I baptized as a result told me, "Yes, I came to Christ in the Graham meeting. But that isn't what brought me to Christ." She then talked about two Christian men from our church with whom she worked at the fire department. She said that observing their Christian life had made her approach them and say, "I need what you've got." So they invited her to their Bible study and then to the Billy Graham meeting.

Likewise, people come to our church, hear an evangelistic sermon, and become Christians because first they've been impressed with the witness and friendship of our members.

Evangelism, then, depends not primarily on the preacher. Certainly, the sermon plays a vital role in the process. But it is a church effort. No one person has to bear the weight of this joyous but formidable task.

Some Elements of Style

The evangelistic sermon has taken many forms over the centuries. Bishop Quayle said that preaching is not so much preparing a sermon and delivering it as it is preparing a preacher and delivering him. In spite of the many changes in time and culture, that remains especially true of evangelistic preaching.

Fundamental to our preparation, of course, is immersion in

prayer and Scripture. But beyond that, I preach more effective evangelistic sermons when I remember the following things.

● *Practice vicarious dialogue.* Evangelism is not a gimmick. It's not some smooth technique of persuasion. Too many people think of the evangelist as a smooth salesman who comes in to sign people up. Instead, when I evangelize, I'm not trying to manipulate people's minds about their deepest needs and questions and sell them the gospel. Rather, I'm simply trying to describe their deepest concerns and show how Jesus addresses them.

I do that by practicing "vicarious dialogue." As I prepare my sermon, I try to listen to the objections and questions my listeners may have at certain points in my message: "Yes, but what about this?" or "Okay, but so what?" Then I craft my sermon to respond to people's questions at appropriate points. This forces me to think seriously about the people I'm addressing. It also helps them see that I am not just trying to get them interested in something they don't care about; I'm responding to their interests.

● *Don't put down; lift up Christ.* Years ago I attended a missions conference in West Pakistan where Bishop Wolmar spoke. It was during the time when many were suggesting we impose a moratorium on foreign missions. Wolmar said, "We will long want missionaries to come to Pakistan, but not the kind who come reaching down to help poor benighted souls. Instead, we want those who will come and stand alongside them, regarding them as sincerely religious, showing them what Jesus offers that they don't have."

Unfortunately, some preachers misrepresent other views, seeking to rebut them, or they ridicule others' opinions. Instead, I try to understand other religions and world views, present them fairly and accurately, and lift Jesus higher.

A friend of mine, David Shenk, who has a doctorate in Islamic studies, does this well in a book he wrote with Islamic scholar Badra Katereqqa: *Islam and Christianity.* David wrote chapters on how the Christian views the Islamic faith; Katereqqa described how the Muslim views the Christian faith. Then they each wrote a response to the other. In the end, they each acknowledged that their disagreement hinged on the Christian idea that God loved us so much that he entered the world in Christ and suffered. For the Muslim that's impossible, for the Christian, essential. In sum, David Shenk didn't try to condemn Islam; he simply showed the Muslim readers the uniqueness of Jesus Christ.

• *Use language that connects.* I was talking once with a man from the inner city of Washington, D.C. When he learned I was a preacher, he asked with a belligerent tone, "Tell me what difference it makes in my life that Jesus died on a cross two thousand years ago."

Fond of theology as I am, I was tempted to describe to him the theological meaning of the atonement. Instead, I said, "Do you have some close friends?" When he nodded yes, I continued, "Suppose one of them gets in trouble. What are you going to do with him?"

"Help him out," he said.

"How long are you going to hang in?"

"Well, he's your friend. You hang in."

"But he gets in worse trouble still. When can you cop out?"

A little peeved, he said, "Man, if he's your friend, you don't cop out. Even criminals won't cop out."

I looked at him and said, "And God came to us as a friend and identified with us in our problem. When can he cop out?"

"You mean Jesus?" he asked.

"Yes. If he's a friend, when can he say, 'That's it. I've gone far enough with you'?"

All at once, lights went on in his eyes, and he said, "You mean that's why Jesus had to die?"

"That's one reason. He couldn't cop out short of death, or else he wasn't really hanging in with you."

He stood up and dusted off his pants. Then he grinned at me and walked off down the street, squaring his shoulders as he went. As I watched him walk away, I muttered to him (although he couldn't hear), "You don't know it, but you've been evangelized."

There's more to the atonement than that, of course. But what I did explain of the atonement, I explained in language this man could identify with. The same sort of thing has to happen for evangelistic preaching to be effective.

Diversifying Our Approach

Effective evangelistic preaching also depends on using a variety of elements.

• *Themes.* All evangelistic preaching aims to bring people to a decision about Christ. We make a mistake, however, if we assume that all evangelistic preaching must begin and end on the same note. Christ meets needs in a variety of ways: he's the propitiation for our sins, yes, but he's also the norm for ethics, the Shepherd of sheep, the Bread of Life, the Way, the Truth, and the Life.

I preached a series of evangelistic sermons in Kansas a few years ago. After the first night's sermon, a woman shook my hand at the door and said, "Thank you for that message. But I didn't hear anything about the blood tonight."

I said, "No, that wasn't my subject."

"In our church," she said, "we hear about the blood in every sermon."

"Well," I said, "you come back tomorrow night."

She did, and she heard about the blood. At the door she shook my hand and thanked me, saying how she appreciated hearing about the blood of Christ. I kept holding her hand and said, "Madam, you do yourself and your pastor a disservice. The gospel has so many elements. If you insist he preach every Sunday on the blood of Christ, he will never get to other themes that could enrich your faith."

• *Needs.* Too many times we fail to recognize that people come to hear us for different reasons. Some people come out of fear of death. Others come out of a sense of emptiness — their lives lack meaning, and they're bored. Some want their salvation assured. Others' lives are in shambles, and they need help. And sometimes people are troubled by their addictions, enslaved to chemicals, ambition, or bad relationships. Preaching is better when adjusted to the needs calling to be addressed.

• *Cultures.* Although largely young, white professionals attend our church, we do have a number of minority groups actively involved. A message that works for one subculture, of course, may not work for another. I need to remember the variety of cultures I address. And it doesn't hurt to get help in doing so.

Sometimes we invite a guest preacher who speaks the language of the black community, or a music group that appeals more to another ethnic subculture. A different part of the neighborhood often turns out for them, one that doesn't come to hear me.

• *Settings.* I get calls from university campuses and community groups to speak or lead in prayer. I often accept these invitations and use them to "preach" evangelistically in a new setting.

I was invited to lead the invocation at a national insurance conference in Washington, D.C. Not all of the conference planners were particularly interested in Christianity, but some were Christians and thought prayer was a good thing to have on the program. So I went to dinner with the group. When they called on me to lead the invocation, I stepped up to the microphone and said, "If I'm going to lead you in prayer, then it's better if you understand where I'm coming from."

Succinctly I indicated that I was a committed Christian. I hadn't come simply as a professional minister who prays for a living, but as one whose walk with Christ is extremely meaningful. I went so far as to invite God to be working in the life of each person at this event. *Then* I led in prayer.

After the program, a number of people came and thanked me, not for the prayer, but for my introductory comments. I rarely do something like that, but in that setting, I felt a touch of evangelism was called for. Naturally, I don't want to misuse such situations. But if handled with tact, we can use them effectively to present Christ to others.

When All Is Said but Not Done: Invitations

It irks me when, after an evangelistic sermon, someone asks, "How many did you get down front?" Evangelism's effectiveness can't be measured that way. Yet in many churches, the altar call remains the measure of the preacher's success. And that can lead to many sorts of manipulation.

I was in one evangelistic meeting when the evangelist closed his message by asking, "How many of you want to love the Lord more? Raise your hand." Of course, we all raised our hands. Then he said, "If you really mean that, stand up." Naturally, a lot of us stood up. Then he said, "If you really mean that, come down front." And a lot of people walked to the front and were taken to a counseling room and prayed for. Later they were reported as people who responded to the invitation. Yet as a listener, I felt manipulated.

So, giving an invitation can be used inappropriately. Yet, I believe at the right time and place it's the right thing to do. It is one way in which people can make a public commitment to Christ.

There are few hard-and-fast guidelines as to the right time and place. Different churches, different pastors, and different sermons will demand different responses.

Sometimes it's far better to let people pray in silence after a sermon, encouraging them to talk to me after the service or during the week. Other times, in planning a public invitation, I make it clear from the beginning where the sermon is heading. Once in a while, I make a judgment in the midst of the service; I didn't plan it, but by the end of the sermon I sense it is appropriate to invite people to make a public response.

Even though the time and place is flexible, there are two things we try to do to make invitations meaningful for the people coming forward.

First, we prepare the people for the invitations. That means sometimes offering invitations in nonevangelistic settings. For instance, after a sermon on Christ's power in our lives, we may invite people to come forward to have an elder pray for them about some area in which they need to experience more of Christ's power. That not only gives Christians an opportunity to be ministered to, it also makes invitations after evangelistic sermons less threatening. Unbelievers who attend our church become aware that in our congregation, it's natural for people to go forward to pray and be helped.

Second, in offering an evangelistic invitation, we try to be clear about the level of commitment we are inviting people to make. If we give a narrow invitation just for unbelievers, spotlighting them unduly, we put those people in a tight spot. They may feel awkward about walking to the front of a congregation of committed Christians. That's an unnecessary social hurdle to expect them to overcome. On the other hand, we don't want to play games with people and make the invitation so general it applies to anyone who wants to do better in life.

The subject of the sermon, of course, will determine to a large degree what we invite people to do. But we try to be as specific as possible without throwing up needless social barriers.

The Fruit of Practicing the Great Commission

In 1980 I spent a year at Princeton Theological Seminary as a scholar-in-residence. Esther and I lived in a seminary apartment during our stay. One of my first mornings there, as I stepped into the hall to get my mail, a young woman approached me and asked, "Are you Dr. Augsburger?" I said I was. "Well, my husband and I live upstairs and I wanted to meet you." Then, just like that, she asked, "Where were you in the summer of 1959?"

I thought a bit and said, "Well, I think I was on an evangelistic mission."

She asked, "Were you in Arthur, Illinois?"

"Yes, I was," I said.

"Do you remember the young Mennonite girl who brought one of her atheist high school friends to talk to you?"

"No," I had to admit, "I don't remember that."

"Well, I was that atheist. We talked for an hour and you gave me all the reasons I should be a Christian. But you didn't push me to make a commitment. When we got up to leave, you turned to me and said, 'Marilyn, I'm sorry for you, because you're going to miss out on so much that Jesus intends for you to enjoy.' "

"Well," she concluded, "I never got away from that."

She had become a Christian. She had earned a doctorate in philosophy and, with her husband, was a guest teacher that year at

Princeton. They're both on the faculty at the University of California. About two years ago, she was ordained in the Episcopal church.

You can see why, then, I remain committed to evangelistic preaching. It's not just because of the Great Commission. It's also because of its great satisfaction.

An atmosphere of warmth and acceptance is expressed most effectively by people who hold no official position. That's because the most gratifying welcome a visitor can receive is from someone he wouldn't expect to welcome him, in a place he didn't expect it to happen.

— Calvin Ratz

CHAPTER TWELVE
Assimilating Newcomers

Newcomers don't come with the glue already applied. It's up to the congregation to make them stick.

But that's easier said than done. Experience shows that not everyone who attends church once wants to return.

Visitors arrive at a church's doorstep for a variety of reasons. There are disgruntled church hoppers, unsaved people genuinely seeking either spiritual or material help, newcomers to town, recent converts, and spiritual prodigals returning to God. Each comes with a different set of fears and expectations. All must be handled carefully if they are going to come back a second time.

At times, church insiders fail to realize how intimidated new-comers feel when attending church. Insiders, familiar with the tra-ditions, the rubrics of worship, the machinery of church programs, and even the layout of their facilities, tend to forget that outsiders see these smoothly flowing activities as intimidating barriers to becoming part of an unfamiliar church.

It's a Big Job

A study by the White House Office of Consumer Affairs indi-cates that 96 percent of dissatisfied business customers never take their complaints to the offending company. In other words, for every complaint a company hears, twenty-four complaints are never received. The study's most frustrating finding, however, is that each of those dissatisfied customers will tell an average of ten friends about the problem. People who attend church aren't much different.

I know the reasons some people stick with our church. Those who've stayed tell me about the friendliness, the opportunities for ministry, and the sense of God's presence in the services. But how do we find out why others never return? Moreover, those who don't return are the worst advertisements for our church in the community.

Churches' track records in getting first-timers back for a sec-ond visit aren't good. One pastor of a church that works meticu-lously to follow up visitors, who even has a secretary assigned to help integrate newcomers, says perhaps 2 to 3 percent of first-timers ever return. Most of us think we're doing better than that, but we probably aren't.

Furthermore, the need to work at assimilation is greater than ever. In particular, denominational loyalty is eroding. One re-searcher discovered that of Christians moving from one city to another, 50 percent switched denominations. Even within a com-munity, there's a shopping mall mentality toward church atten-dance. People "go where the action is," regardless of denominational affiliation. That means transfers aren't assured.

And assimilating newcomers involves much more than placing warm, friendly greeters at the door. It's spiritual conflict. The Devil doesn't want people in the church, and with a variety of subtle innuendoes and imagined thoughts, he works to make people feel they don't belong. He's constantly pulling people away, not only from God, but from the church. Assimilation needs to be a matter of prayer.

It's hard to define a successful rate of assimilation. The apostle Paul didn't keep everyone. Some who heard him came back only to throw stones. We need to accept without rancor the fact that not all will consider our church worth joining. That's only realistic. But I don't want to be the cause of someone's not returning. Although we'll never meet everyone's needs, we can work to make newcomers feel welcome and to arouse social and spiritual appetites that make them want to return.

Our family has attended many kinds of churches while on vacation. In the car after a service, I've frequently asked, "If we lived nearby, would you want to go back to that church?" I've heard mixed responses. When I've asked why, I've received a string of answers:

"Everyone seemed so happy."

"Unfriendly."

"No sense of God's presence."

"The place was alive. Everyone was involved."

"I didn't know the words to the music."

"No one showed us where to go!"

"The preacher was cold."

"The preacher told some great stories."

"I felt like everyone was looking at us all the time!"

Looking back at scores of churches I've visited, I've classified three broad factors that determine a newcomer's willingness to return. In management terms, they are "the critical success factors": obstacles, atmosphere, and structure.

Obstacles to Assimilation

A church's composition, history, or philosophy of ministry can throw up a wall newcomers have a difficult time scaling. Here are some of the situations a congregation may face that can place barriers before newcomers.

• *Large family networks.* In our church, three family circles with a chain of relationships connect more than 175 people. These networks have their own social gatherings in which outsiders aren't included. The Thanksgiving dinner table has little space for strangers. These families enjoy built-in care. News about needs spreads internally, apart from the church. Relatives often are so busy taking care of family needs, little time remains to consider the needs of outsiders. Such networks can be deadly to assimilating newcomers.

We've done two things to deal with this issue. First, we tactfully alerted some in these families to the potential problems, challenging them to take care to include outsiders in some of their social gatherings. Second, we've outgrown the family circles with new growth, so they no longer dominate our fellowship.

• *Existing friendships.* The fellowship of churches known for friendliness and care can sometimes be difficult to crack. If the energy of the congregation is given to caring for existing members rather than identifying the needs of newcomers, love becomes ingrown.

Even pulpit statements about friendliness can irritate newcomers. I remember visiting one church and hearing the pastor talk about their friendliness. The church *was* friendly. I watched people in animated conversations with their friends, but the whole time, I sat alone on the pew feeling like an ice cube. No one talked with me. The pastor's comments and the excited conversations around me only accentuated the fact I was an outsider and didn't belong. A time for greeting newcomers would have structured a way for that church to share the warmth outside already-established circles.

• *Facilities.* The design of church buildings, especially poor layout of the foyer and other entrances, can be an obstacle to a newcomer's welcome. In some churches even *finding* the sanctuary is a challenge. No signs direct you to entrances, the nursery, or rest rooms. Such inconsideration makes newcomers uncomfortable. Indirectly, but forcefully, the church is saying to visitors, "We weren't expecting you."

However, facilities *can* communicate warmth and friendliness. In order to create a feeling of intimacy in a large, old building, one small congregation removed the pews, placed padded chairs in a cozy arrangement, and brought the platform closer to the congregation. These people knew a small congregation in a large room makes newcomers feel uncomfortable, so they contrived an intimate atmosphere, even in a cavernous space.

People respond to crowded facilities in a variety of ways. Some outsiders interpret a full sanctuary as a good sign. They think, *Something's happening here, and I want to be a part of it!* Others see it as an indication there's no room for them and they aren't needed. Researchers believe a congregation generally won't grow above 85 percent of the sanctuary seating capacity. Unless the church is a going concern in a generally lackluster spiritual community, a packed sanctuary communicates, "We don't care to make room for you."

● *A church's history.* Some congregations seem more interested in the past than in the future. Sermon illustrations and announcements constantly refer to past events and cherished traditions. Continual references to names of former members and leaders are meaningless to outsiders and say the church is more interested in its past heroes than in newcomers.

Even excessive denominationalism can hinder assimilation. People seeking help today don't go to a church because it belongs to a historic denomination. They go because they believe they will receive help.

What people seek is a refreshing alternative to the world outside. No one returns for a second visit because a denominational flag has been waved; they come back because they experienced God's presence and the acceptance of God's people.

● *Special events.* Some folk fail to stick because the event that first attracted them to the church is not the regular diet of the church. For example, a guest musician may pull in a crowd, but the crowd he attracts comes with taste buds for a certain type of music. If the church doesn't deliver that type of ministry on a regular basis, the person feels hungry.

Generally, people expect as a norm the kind of ministry that first attracted them to a church. This, of course, is one of the major problems in integrating new converts who've come through TV and radio ministries. Normal church life doesn't match expectations caused by the media ministry. People attracted to a church by special events likely will stick only if the kind of ministry that first attracted them is sustained — a difficult undertaking.

• *Philosophy of ministry.* If the pastor or congregation believes church life is generated from the platform on Sunday morning, integration means getting as many people into the sanctuary for Sunday mornings as possible. In such situations, allegiance is to the pastor and not the congregation. Both strong pulpiteers and flamboyant personalities can build a following, but they may be only attracting a crowd, not assimilating members into a church body.

If, however, a church's ministry emphasizes interaction among members and shared ministry, integration means providing facilities and programs for people to build friendships and to become involved in service. Church life is what happens among members, as well as in the public worship service.

A woman was converted and started attending our services regularly. Her husband drove her to church each week and picked her up afterward. The first time he attended a service at our church, he said, "You people are so different. You never want to leave the church. Church is something you do together. In my church, I go to Mass as a stranger. I can be a good Catholic and not know anyone else in the church, let alone talk to anyone. You can't do that in your church!"

Ministry of the body is as important as ministry on the platform, not only for nurturing the saints, but also for assimilating new members.

• *A reputation of tension.* Strife between members is picked up quickly by newcomers. And animosity is a poor advertisement. Newcomers want no part of a church torn by dissension.

A while back I was called to mediate a church fight in a small but divided congregation. A visitor from that community who had attended just one service told me about his icy reception and how both sides viewed him suspiciously. During the following week he was visited by members of both sides in the dispute, each trying to recruit him to their side. Naturally, he never went back.

The answer, of course, is an emphasis on forgiveness and reconciliation. A torn church cannot weave in new members. Until strife becomes the exception rather than the way of life, the church cannot expect to attract and hold new members.

• *Confusing service styles.* Visitors often feel uneasy when they first attend church. They're on strange turf. Much of what we do in our services, though familiar to members, is intimidating to visitors. An expressive worship style frightens someone who doesn't understand; a highly liturgical service loses the uninitiated. Choruses sung without a hymnal exclude newcomers unless the words are printed in the bulletin or projected on a screen.

Our Sunday morning service includes the reading of Scripture. While most of our people bring their Bibles, visitors often don't. Therefore, we print the Scripture passage in the bulletin so outsiders aren't excluded. (It also solves the "Which translation?" issue.)

Offerings may make visitors suspect that the church only wants money. So, during the offering at special events, where we have a significant number of outsiders, I usually say, "If you are a visitor, you're our guest, and there's no obligation for you to participate in the offering. However, this is one way the people of our own congregation express their worship to God."

Even during our recent building program, I said little about money from the pulpit. Our special appeals were made primarily through literature we mailed. Many people new to our church have commented on how they were initially impressed by our financial discretion.

• *Class and cultural distinctions.* There are rich and poor people. There are retirement communities, university communities, and working-class communities. There are farm towns, inner-city ghettos, and suburbs. People aren't all the same. Even if they speak English, they don't all talk the same language. And while those differences shouldn't affect how people interact, they do make a difference in how comfortable outsiders feel when they come into a church.

Some churches try to be all things to all people. But most churches have difficulty providing an environment in which everyone feels comfortable. Usually one social culture dominates.

The solution is to sensitize insiders, gently and consistently, to the need to make everyone welcome, while recognizing that a church's growth likely will reflect its cultural and social composition.

• *Poor attitudes.* Perhaps the greatest obstacle to newcomers' integration is the attitude of insiders. Not everyone is as blunt as one person who told me, "Pastor, our church is big enough. We really don't need any more folk in our church!"

Negative attitudes toward outsiders come from many quarters. Church power brokers, fearing a threat to their power base, may resist newcomers. Existing members can resent the financial cost of providing space and staff to care for the needs of newcomers. Church pioneers can withdraw emotional support from the church. No matter how strong the appeal from the leadership, such attitudes, even if expressed by few, freeze newcomers out of the church.

We sensitize the congregation to newcomers by including them on church committees. Obviously senior leadership positions require a record of faithfulness in the church. However, we've worked at including at least one relatively new person on as many committees as possible. The new persons' interaction in the committees is a refreshing reminder to oldtimers that newcomers think differently and must be taken into consideration.

All these obstacles hinder assimilation. Not every church will suffer from all these problems, but every church does well to consider which might be insidiously holding back the integration of newcomers as productive and growing members.

An Atmosphere of Acceptance

Another critical factor in holding newcomers is atmosphere. Some churches exude an atmosphere that says, "Visitors are welcome here." It doesn't derive from handouts or slogans. It's not particularly what happens up front, though that helps. It's an air that permeates the whole congregation, an intangible that says to first-timers, "We've been expecting you, and we're glad you've come."

Growing churches are service oriented rather than product oriented. In the words of Ken Blanchard, author of *The One Minute Manager*, "Large and small companies alike are learning that in today's competitive marketplace, it is often good service — not product superiority or low pricing — that determines success." In other words, it's not the companies with the best products that succeed, it's those who take the best care of their customers that become profitable.

The same can be said of the church. Growing churches make a commitment to meet the needs of newcomers. They create an environment where everything is designed with the newcomer's experience in mind. They remember the humanness of their visitors.

As the pastor assigned to do most of the preaching, I can become so caught up in sermon preparation and delivery that I forget the needs of the very people the sermon addresses. That's like a quarterback trying to complete a pass while eyeing the scoreboard. The sermon and other aspects of the church's ministry need to focus on the quality of the newcomer's social and spiritual experiences, providing the subtle yet overriding message: "Newcomers are wanted and needed here."

How is that done? For one, by pastors when they tune vocabulary to outsiders; when ordinances are explained in the language of nonchurched people; when the leadership style is warm, personable, and conversational. There's what a friend of mine calls "pastoring from the pulpit."

He says he accomplishes in those moments some of the pastoral care he is unable to achieve throughout the week. He also says it's the time in the service when visitors come alive. His vulnerability and openness as he chats pastorally with the congregation partially breaks down the barrier between the pew and pulpit that newcomers often feel.

The atmosphere of warmth and acceptance, however, is expressed most effectively by people who hold no official position. That's because the most gratifying welcome a visitor can receive is from someone he wouldn't expect to welcome him, in a place he didn't expect it to happen. It may be a warm comment by the person in the next pew. It might be several smiles and a lot of eye contact in the foyer before the service. Certainly there's touch. We may not kiss as they did in New Testament days, but at least as the Phillips translation puts it, there should be "a handshake all around!" Welcoming isn't just something done at the door; it's something *everyone* does all over the building.

Such an atmosphere can't be structured, but it can be fostered. Here are some things we encourage to create an atmosphere of warmth.

We have men directing traffic on our parking lot as people arrive for services. This not only heads off a lot of confusion, it also tells newcomers we want to make it easy for them to find their way. There's a warm smile even before people get out of their cars.

Several people are assigned to minister in the church foyer. Our greeters shake as many hands as possible. Others, our hosts and hostesses, watch especially for visitors. They're prepared to answer visitors' questions and to give directions. They also attempt to get first-timers to sign the guest book or a visitor's card. We also have a staffed information counter. In addition, we train our ushers how to be friendly and sensitive to outsiders.

Assigning at least one or two staff members to serve in the foyer — before, during, and after every service — has been our most productive means of identifying and welcoming visitors. The presence of a pastor in the foyer models the atmosphere we want. In fact, the staff person primarily responsible for the integration of newcomers has been dubbed "pastor of the foyer."

Two other methods help foster the atmosphere we seek. First, I talk about visitors often. I use them in sermon illustrations. I remind the congregation how uncomfortable visitors may feel. I liken our congregation to the staff of a large department store. We're there to serve newcomers.

Second, during a time for greeting in our services, we suggest people welcome at least six to eight people. I encourage people to start their greeting with the words, "Hi! I'm ———." There's something personable about a first name. It also saves embarrassment by helping people learn the names of others in the congregation.

Structured to Include

What happens if people like the atmosphere of a congregation but then find no group of people with whom they can relate? Churches of all sizes share this woe. Small churches sometimes become cliquish or ingrown. Larger churches may seem impersonal, making the newcomer feel insignificant.

But this need not be a problem if a structure is in place to identify and place newcomers into smaller groupings in which they can minister and find a place of belonging.

Several years ago we adopted Peter Wagner's concept of "celebration, congregation, and cell." Basically, the idea is that the Sunday morning celebration can continue to grow indefinitely if two other groupings exist within the church. In addition to the Sunday celebration (everybody gathered for worship), there needs to be a number of both congregations (a subgrouping of forty to one hundred people) and small, intimate cells (informal networks of friends; intimate, task-oriented groups; or structured small-group gatherings).

We've paid particular attention to building the *congregations;* they've been invaluable for integrating newcomers. These groupings are large enough not to intimidate newcomers, yet small enough for them to get to know others. We're convinced that if we can get newcomers into one of these congregations, there's a high probability they'll remain in our web of love.

We have about thirty of these congregations, some based on fellowship, some on special interests, and some on ministry. For instance, each of the choirs is a congregation. The workers of many of our programs also become little congregations in which there is a network of friendships and accountability.

Our most important congregations for integrating newcomers are our age-divided adult fellowship groups. We've divided our church by ten-year age spans and placed each person in one of these congregations. Each has its own lay leader and committee as well as its own pastor. These groups meet weekly as Sunday school classes, hold regular social activities, and provide a caring ministry for the needy within the group.

But how do we channel people into these congregations?

Assimilating churches build structures that ensure newcomers are identified, cared for, and integrated into the fabric of the church. Here's how we go about it.

● *Identifying newcomers.* We identify newcomers in a variety of ways. Counselors fill in response cards for those who respond to an altar call. Greeters and hosts get names, and addresses if possible. They're trained to write down the names so they're not forgotten. During services we ask each visitor to fill in an information card. Pastors working in the foyer carry visitor cards that they fill in on the spot.

Some newcomers don't want to be spotlighted; it's the anonymity of a larger church that attracts them in the first place. So we try not to overpower them. But we know that if we don't get a name and phone number or address, our chances of holding and helping visitors is greatly diminished.

One yardstick of success for a Sunday is the number of new names and addresses of first-timers we garner. New names and addresses are our prime contacts for ministry through the week. Without those names and addresses, midweek ministry to newcomers suffers.

One interesting source of information about newcomers is our offering envelopes. It's amazing that with all our efforts to contact visitors, some are missed. Yet some not only keep attending, they also start using offering envelopes! Our bookkeeper alerts us to these people.

● *Making midweek contact.* Follow-up ministry starts Monday morning. My secretary helps me send a letter of welcome to every visitor. For a while, we didn't send the letter to out-of-town visitors, but now we do. We discovered some out-of-towners were in the process of moving to our city, and it was important to give these visitors a feeling that they were noticed and appreciated.

A staff member processes these names on Monday and Tuesday. He makes an initial phone call, welcoming the people to our church and asking if it would be possible for someone from the church to make a call at the home. He attempts to gain further information, such as the approximate age of the adults and ages of children. He completes a family information form as the call is being made.

Following the call, this pastor may visit the family or assign it to one of the other pastors. He matches the family with the most suitable staff member, taking into account age, spiritual need, and special interests.

Copies of the family information sheet are shared during our staff meeting on Wednesday mornings. From that point, one pastor is assigned and responsible for each newcomer. In addition, we see that the appropriate lay leaders in the youth department, ministry programs, and Sunday school are notified of the new family.

Each of our adult fellowship groups has lay members who assist in the ministry of integration. Each pastor works with his lay leaders to watch for recent newcomers on Sunday, make midweek contact, invite them to informal coffee gatherings, and introduce them to other members of the class.

• *Maintaining a newcomers' directory.* We keep all newcomers in a separate directory for six months. This list is reviewed at staff meetings, and pastors report on people's progress. After six months on the list, a decision is made to (1) place the name in the church directory as an assimilated family, (2) delete the name as someone unlikely to come back, or (3) leave the name on the newcomers list for another six months since their status is still undetermined.

• *Providing a "Welcome to the Family Class."* This class is an invaluable tool for making newcomers feel a part of the church. It's promoted as a class for all newcomers, not just new converts.

I lead this class during the Sunday school hour. We believe newcomers are attracted to a class led by someone with a high profile in the worship service. Two lay couples also work with me, befriending and encouraging newcomers.

The class is a relaxed and informal opportunity to get acquainted. Over coffee, we try to make newcomers feel at ease in the church. The content of the class varies depending on who is present. We spend a great deal of time prompting and then answering questions about what we believe and how our church functions. Over a six- to eight-week period, we cover the basic teachings and practices of the church.

I spend considerable time outlining how the church functions and how to build church friendships. Mostly, I watch for specific needs, spiritual problems, and questions newcomers may have. Through our lay leaders, we reach out to meet these needs. We strongly encourage people to become involved in the church's activities, stressing that friendships are built as a byproduct of doing things together.

After someone has attended the class about two months, our lay leaders introduce the person to the lay leaders of the appropriate adult fellowship group and the pastor assigned to that group. Responsibility for integration is passed from the Welcome to the Family Class to the adult fellowship group. Newcomers are encouraged to attend Sunday school.

Each convert is encouraged also to attend one of the midweek home fellowship groups especially designed for new Christians. Each newcomer who is not a new Christian is introduced to the leader or host of one of our regular Neighborhood Bible Study groups.

• *Integrating into ministry.* We believe it's critical for newcomers to become involved in the church's ministry as quickly as possible. In fact, we feel that until newcomers assume some ministry responsibility, they won't feel emotionally one with us. They will think of the church as "them" rather than "us."

Newcomers must not feel only wanted, they also must feel

needed. Some people think that as a church grows larger, there's less opportunity to be involved in ministry. That's just not the case. A while back, we surveyed our congregational involvement in ministry and discovered there were 995 ministry jobs being done by 602 people. That's a vast army. Yet we easily could use another 150 workers today.

The key is to let the newcomer become involved in meaningful ministry. I want newcomers to expect to make a significant contribution to our ministries.

So we talk regularly about ministry opportunities. We highlight what's being done. We share our vision. We explain the diversity of ways people can become involved. Though critical recruiting is done individually, from time to time we encourage the congregation to fill in a ministry opportunity sheet. These sheets are of little value for longstanding members, but they give newcomers an opportunity to express their interests.

The Ones Who Stick

Some people don't want to be integrated into any church. They may lack a basic commitment to God, and no amount of friendliness will make them stay. Others bear the imprint of our culture that recoils from commitment to anything.

Such people drift through every congregation. Seeing them fall away can be disappointing, especially when we work so hard to show them the challenge and benefits of commitment to a local church.

The thrill of pastoring, however, is to look over a congregation on Sunday morning and see the people who have come and been helped and assimilated.

— Glen decided to become a Christian at a drama presentation. Today, he's an usher.

— Phyllis was delivered from an oppressive spiritual environment. Today she works in one of our children's ministries.

— Paul accepted Christ in my office. He's active in the church with his wife and two children.

— Russ and Cathy prayed for forgiveness and salvation with me in a restaurant over lunch. They became involved in our sound ministry.

— Ed and Karen felt they were part of the church when they were asked to serve on one of our adult fellowship committees.

These special souls — and a host of others — are all part of each Sunday's celebration. They're there, not because of a specific program but as a result of an entire congregation spinning a web of love — a web that helps newcomers stick.

Using the Bible as an uncompromising foundation, these men have effectively employed the capital their situation handed them. They are, in the best sense of the term, missionary entrepreneurs.

— Mark Galli

Epilogue

ntentionally model for others, as you would have them intentionally model for you."

"Have this mind among you: a marketplace mentality."

"Love your target group as yourself."

New commandments? No, just biblical teaching applied to the 1990s by three faithful churches.

For some, of course, the new language of outreach and evangelism sounds like a foreign tongue: "Can't we just get back to the straightforward concepts of the Bible? Do we really need all this stuff to share the love of Christ?" They are bothered because mission described this way seems such a bother.

Others are excited by new vocabulary and eagerly employ it in board meetings and sermons, whether it applies to their situation or not. It makes them feel they're on the cutting edge.

In our discussions about this book, these three authors have impressed me precisely because they are not interested in being on the cutting edge. They yearn, though, to share the love of Christ effectively. And they are not afraid of experimenting with words, ideas, and programs to make that happen.

They are not, of course, "intentionally modeling" any specific technique or ministry idea. If you tried to follow every bit of advice in this book, you'd end up in a mental ward. Frank Tillapaugh pastors an unconventional church in mile-high Denver. Calvin Ratz has a more traditional, but charismatic outreach ministry in reserved British Columbia. Myron Augsburger helps lead an inner-city church in the heart of troubled Washington, D.C. Naturally, their ideas don't always neatly mesh.

But their passion does. More than anything, they model a burning concern to reach those who do not yet know Christ's love. Using the Bible as an uncompromising foundation, they've effectively employed the capital their situation handed them. They are, in the best sense of the term, missionary entrepreneurs, pastors willing to risk and invest themselves that Christ might be known.

And that's a model worth following. Or, as Jesus might have said, "And you shall be my witnesses in Judea, in Samaria, and in all the spheres of evangelistic influence."